Bostick -
Clemson -

Do we as Southern
men know the negro?

Maybry

NEGRO LIFE
IN THE SOUTH

*PRESENT CONDITIONS
AND NEEDS*

BY
W. D. WEATHERFORD, Ph.D.

REVISED EDITION

NEW YORK
ASSOCIATION PRESS
1915

DEDICATED TO THE COLLEGE MEN OF
THE SOUTH, IN WHOSE TOLERANT
SPIRIT AND UNSELFISH INTEREST
LIES THE HOPE OF THE NEGRO RACE.

PREFACE

During the month of April, 1908, a company of seven men, four negroes and three white men, came together in the City of Atlanta to discuss the present race question, with special reference to what the college men of the South might do to better conditions. Those present in this conference were Dr. W. R. Lambuth, Missionary Secretary of the Methodist Episcopal Church, South; Dr. Stewart R. Roberts, formerly a professor at Emory College, Georgia, now professor of physiology in the Atlanta School of Physicians and Surgeons; President John Hope, of Atlanta Baptist College (colored), a colored man of broad education and scholarly spirit; Professor John Wesley Gilbert, one of the most scholarly and sane minded negro men in the South; Messrs. W. A. Hunton and J. E. Moorland, secretaries of the Colored Department, International Committee of Young Men's Christian Associations, and the author.

We spent six hours in a very thorough and earnest conference, the result being a unanimous vote to have a text book prepared on the negro in the South, which could be used in the Home Mission classes of the College Young Men's Christian Associations. The task of preparing this text book was placed upon the author by this committee.

It may be worth while to say that the author is a Southern man, a graduate of Vanderbilt University, and, since leaving college, has been the Student Secretary of the International Committee of Young Men's Christian Associations for the South. It will thus appear that this volume has been prepared by one who has spent his life in the midst of the conditions about which he attempts to write. He, therefore, has no reason to be prejudiced for or against the negro any more than should any other Christian man of the section, save wherein a thorough study of conditions may have brought new convictions.

It is difficult always to think calmly and to speak without passion on a problem such as this, but a deliberate attempt has been made to state the facts in all fairness and calmness. It is believed that the educated men of the South will be glad to study these facts in the same spirit. In them alone do we have any large hope, for most of the untrained men are too full of prejudice to face fairly or solve justly such a momentous question. On the college men, therefore, rests the burden of responsibility in this matter.

If this little volume arouses new interest, and stimulates such careful study as will help toward the proper solution of this, the nation's greatest problem, the writer will be more than satisfied.

W. D. WEATHERFORD.

Nashville, Tenn.,
June, 1, 1910.

CONTENTS

I

WHY STUDY THE NEGRO QUESTION?

THE DESERTED PLANTATION

Oh, de grubbin'-hoe's a-rustin' in de co'nah,
　　An' de plow's a-tumblin' down in de fiel',
While de whippo'will's a-wailin' lak a mou'nah
　　When his stubbo'n hea't is tryin' ha'd to yiel'.

In de furrers whah de co'n was allus wavin',
　　Now de weeds is growin' green an' rank an' tall;
An' de swallers roun' de whole place is a-bravin'
　　Lak dey thought deir folks had allus owned it all.

An' de big house stan's all quiet lak an' solemn,
　　Not a blessed soul in pa'lor, po'ch, er lawn;
Not a guest, ner not a ca'iage lef' to haul 'em,
　　Fu' de ones dat tu'ned de latch-string out air gone.

An' de banjo's voice is silent in de qua'ters,
　　D'ain't a hymn ner co'n-song ringin' in de air;
But de murmur of a branch's passin' waters
　　Is de only soun' dat breks de stillness dere.

Whah's de da'kies, dem dat used to be a-dancin'
　　Ev'ry night befo' de ole cabin do'?
Whah's de chillun, dem dat used to be a-prancin'
　　Er a-rollin' in de san' er on de flo'?

Whah's ole Uncle Mordecai an' Uncle Aaron?
　　Whah's Aunt Doshy, Sam, an' 'Kit, an' all de res'?
Whah's ole Tom de da'ky fiddlah, how's he farin'?
　　Whah's de gals dat used to sing an' dance de bes'?

Gone! Not one o' dem is lef' to tell de story;
　　Dey have lef' de deah ole place to fall away.
Couldn't one o' dem dat seed it in its glory
　　Stay to watch it in de hour of decay?

Dey have lef' de ole plantation to de swallers,
　　But it hol's in me a lover till de las';
Fu' I fin' hyeah in de memory dat follers
　　All dat loved me an' dat I loved in de pas'.

So I'll stay an' watch de deah ole place an' tend it
　　Ez I used to in de happy days gone by.
'Twell do othah Mastah thinks it's time to end it,
　　An' calls me to my quarters in de sky.
　　　　　　　　　　　　　—PAUL LAURENCE DUNBAR.

WHY STUDY THE NEGRO QUESTION?

Foreword

In a time like ours when there are so many vital subjects demanding attention, and every subject is represented by many books, it is only legitimate that men should ask, "Why study the race question?" If it is not a question of first importance, if it does not have to do with our daily lives, if it does not vitally affect our physical, intellectual or moral well-being separately or collectively, then there can be no urgent necessity for the study of this question. If, on the other hand, it can be shown that this race problem enters into every relationship in Southern life, if it can be shown that our health, our intellectual advancement, and our moral lives are hedged about and often limited by the disease, the ignorance, and the immorality of another race; and if it can be further shown that we, as Christian college men, have an opportunity to better these conditions, we will have a sufficient reason for the study of so difficult a question.

Our Ignorance of the Facts

My first answer to why we should study this question is, that we, as Southern college men, are woefully ignorant of the facts. It has been said hundreds of times in print and from the platform that this question cannot be handled by the Northern man, because he is hundreds of miles removed from the scene of action, and does not know the facts. I believe that most of the Northern men are coming to accept the truth of this statement, and most of the best informed negroes, such as Booker T. Washington, are saying plainly that the North does not and cannot know, at least under present conditions, the real race problem. With this first statement, there is always coupled the second, that the Southern white man does know and can therefore solve the Southern race question. I deliberately challenge this statement. I feel perfectly sure that we, as Southern white men, know much more of real negro life than men of other sections can possibly know; I feel sure also of the fact that the best and more broad minded men of the South are more intensely interested in this question than men in any other section can possibly be; and I further feel sure that this question, if ever solved, must be solved by the broad minded Southern men leading the way and calling to their aid the broad minded and philanthropic men of all the nation. But do we as Southern men know the negro?

Knowledge of Servant Class Only

We know the negro as a hired servant in our homes. We know Aunt Mary, who cooks our meals, who waits on our table or acts as housemaid in our homes. We know John, the butler, or the coachman, or the gardener. We know the day laborer who cleans the street or hauls the coal, or runs the grocery wagon. We know one or two negro men who, because of more intelligence, have positions as mail carriers, and perhaps we know half a dozen negroes who, because of skill and hard work, have entered the list of skilled employment. But all of these we know only in their work. We do not know their thought; we do not know their religious life; we do not know their home life.

The Church, the Home, the School

Probably the three best indices of the real character of a people are their religion, their schools and their homes. Of the religious life of the negro, we, as Southern men, know almost nothing. Most of us have not visited half a dozen negro churches in our lives, and then only as onlookers, rather than attempting to enter into the spirit of the service and trying to find its real message. Neither have we studied their school life. We have passed the negro school house every day of our lives, have seen the negro college perched on the hill, but never have we visited these places more than once or twice to see what was actually going on in them. It has never occurred to most of us that these school buildings have anything of interest for us, and nine cases out of ten we do not know the negro preacher or the negro teacher who presides over the nearest church or school. Neither do we know the home life of the negro. I have again and again asked groups of college men how many negro homes they had ever entered.

I have rarely ever found men who had been in more than two or three or half a score at the most. Even where men have gone into negro homes, they have been of the poorer type. It has been the home of the washwoman, the cook or the servant man. The real life of the negro we do not know. There is much justice, though it hurts us as Southern men to admit it, in the statement of Ray Stannard Baker, after his careful and, on the whole, fair minded observations of conditions in the South:

"But, curiously enough, I found that these men rarely knew anything about the better class of negroes—those who were in business, or in independent occupations, those who owned their own homes. They did come into contact with the servant negro, the field hand, the common laborer, who make up, of course, the great mass of the race. On the other hand, the best class of negroes did not know the higher class of white people, and based their suspicion and hatred upon the acts of the poorer sort of whites, with whom they naturally come into contact. The best elements of the two races are as far apart as if they lived in different continents; and that is one of the chief causes of the growing danger in the Southern situation. It is a striking fact that one of the first—almost instinctive—efforts at reconstruction after the Atlanta riot was to bring the best element of both races together, so that they might, by becoming acquainted and gaining confidence in each other, allay suspicion and bring influence to bear on the lawless elements of both white people and colored."[1]

It is not fair to judge a race by its weaker exponents alone, neither is it fair to judge a race simply by one aspect of its life. We must know its whole life before we can claim to know the race. If we are to have a right to speak with any authority on this race question, and if we are to have our proper share in bringing about a true race adjustment, we will need to study with care all the essential activities of this race. To what other group of men can this appeal be so fairly made, and from what other group of men should there be such ready response as from college men?

Self-Preservation

Again, it is important that we study this question, because only a thorough knowledge of the situation will enable us to take such steps as will insure our own safety—physical, mental and moral. However carefully we may guard our contact with the negro—and no sane white man in the South, and few, if any, sane negroes believe in promiscuous mingling—there can be no doubt that the destiny of the Southern white man is inextricably intertwined with that of the Southern black man. Whatever affects one, affects the other, whether we want it so or not.

Health Relations

Every day we put our health in the hands of the negro, because he cooks our meals, washes our

[1] "Following the Color Line," p. 44.

linen, cleans our homes, and nurses our children. If he is clean and healthy, it is well with us; if he is unclean and diseased, woe be to the white man whom he serves. Recently a malignant epidemic of typhoid fever broke out in an Alabama female college. A number of girls died, many others were in bed for weeks and months, some of them will never be so well again. Prof. William Litterer, bacteriologist of Vanderbilt University, Medical Department, was asked to make an investigation of the cause of the epidemic, and after an exhaustive search the infection was traced to a negro boy employed as a dishwasher, "who was a walking arsenal of typhoid germs." Those mothers and fathers who lost their daughters in this epidemic would be easily convinced that it is worth while to make a careful study of the race problem with the purpose of seeing to it that there is better sanitation and health conditions among the negroes who work in our homes. Whether we sit down to dinner in our home or in a hotel, it is a vital question which cannot lightly be passed over—under what sanitary conditions does the negro who cooked this meal and the negro who served it live? To be indifferent to the health question of the negro is to be indifferent to the sickness and disease which may rob us of our health or the health and life of our own loved ones.

Intellectual Relations

This is equally true of the intellectual life of the Southern white man. We are bound down and hedged about by the ignorance of our servants and our laboring class. Not long since a college president was writing to me about a college graduate who wanted a place in Young Men's Christian Association work, and in his letter he apologized for the poor English of this student in the following words: "His weakest spot is his spoken English, as he grew up in a community so thickly populated by negroes that he has never been able to shake off some of the dialect." It is probably impossible ever to estimate just how much of a handicap are the superstitions, the prejudices and the ignorant fears, which are being daily poured into the minds of Southern childhood by the ignorant servant class. In simple self-defence, we must see to it that the negroes are freed from at least the grosser forms of ignorance and superstition.

Moral Contagion

Nor can we escape the moral contagion of close contact with those who are morally leprous. The latest word of psychology and sociology is that character is not taught but character is caught. Character is as contagious as measles or confluent smallpox. Henry Drummond once said: "I become a part of every man I meet, and every man I meet becomes a part of me." Almost every child in the well-to-do Southern home is more in the companionship of the nurse than of the mother, up to the age of six—that is, during those very impressionable days when character is just taking shape. Even in the less wealthy homes, the

child is constantly thrown into the presence of
the servants, and if these servants be immoral
in any sense, the consequent detriment of character is sure.

The constant presence of those who are impure and immoral means the gradual lowering
of ideals, the deadening of conscience, the loss of
the sense of sin. Who of us has not seen just
such a process going on in a Southern household?

No Arraignment of Servants

These words are not written as an arraignment
of negro servants, for I am well aware that
hundreds of servants are honest and true, and
while they are usually ignorant as to books, they
not infrequently have that truer knowledge
gained from contact with life, and, at the same
time, that unselfishness of spirit and genuineness
of soul which makes them a real blessing to
the home in which they work. But so long as
there are many of the opposite type, so long as
there are many who live in unsanitary hovels and
are filthy in body, ignorant and superstitious in
mind, and leprous in soul—just so long will they
be a plague to our Southern white people. In
the interest of self-defence, every intelligent
white man must study this question, and be prepared to take his part in the physical, social, intellectual, and moral regeneration of this neglected race.

Race Antagonism

Again, there is need of study of this question
because of the growing spirit of race antagonism

and unrest. That there is such an antagonism in certain sections can hardly be denied. The reasons for this are not far to seek. The passing away of the old-time darkey with his simplicity, love of the plantation, and devotion to the people of the "big house," the rise of the younger negro, with less respect, with less ability as a trained workman, with possibly less disposition to work; the rise also of the educated negro class, sometimes arrogant, always and rightly more independent; the passing of the old plantation owners who knew the negro far better than the present generation of white men; these have made possible less and less of real understanding between the two races, and have brought on many conditions of friction. Besides these natural causes of race antagonism, there have been three classes of men who have piled fuel on the fire and fanned the smouldering embers into flame.

Prejudiced Southern White Man

The first is that class of Southern white men who are utterly incapable of seeing anything good in the negro. I met one of them not long since—a physician—who in one breath declared hell was too good for the negro criminal, and in the next breath claimed the negro had no soul. He was somewhat surprised and seemed not to catch the point when I asked him if he thought his horse would go to hell because in a fit of ill temper he kicked his master. But the more dangerous Southern white man is he who mounts the political stump and with wild gesticulations cries, "Social Equality," "Negro Domination," "Race Amalgamation," and such other blood curdling shibboleths, and so stirs up such a race antagonism that men forget all about the real political issues, and the demagogue rides into office, at the expense of justice to the negro and the self-respect of the white man. *We have had all too many of these political demagogues— these so-called "defenders of the white man's honor and the white woman's virtue."* It is high time that the college should know enough about this question not to be browbeaten and befogged into supporting any such cheap gerrymanderism.

The Radical Negro

The second man who stirs up race hatred is the radical negro, and I am sorry to say he frequently comes from the ranks of the educated. This type of man finds his best expression through the "Niagara Movement," organized by Prof. W. E. B. DuBois, the express object of which is to continually protest against all forms of discrimination. Its purpose seems not to be the helping of the colored race to be worthy of position, but the stirring up of that race to demand and take certain so-called rights. The public exponent of this ideal has been the "Guardian," published by William Monroe Trotter, in Boston. This group of men is hot in its denunciation of Booker T. Washington, because he believes in conciliation and constructive work. They believe that the whole *régime* of the present is wrong and should be destroyed. This attitude toward Washington is best displayed in a reference to him by Professor DuBois: "So thoroughly did he (Washington) learn the speech and thought of triumphant commercialism, and the ideals of material prosperity, that the picture of a lone black boy poring over a French grammar amid the weeds and dirt of a neglected home soon seemed to him the acme of absurdities. One wonders what Socrates and St. Francis of Assisi would say to this . . . It is as though Nature must make men narrow in order to give them force."[1]

These men can as little see any virtue in a Southern white man as the Southern demagogue can see virtue in the negro. I cannot better convey the spirit of bitterness and hatred of this radical negro wing than to give one or two quotations from some of its leaders: "In general," says William A. Sinclair—a South Carolina negro and a college graduate—"a spirit of cruel intolerance dominates the white population of the whole Southland. Its church life, despite the many excellent and truly Christian members, both men and women, betrays strange deformities and inconsistencies; in large measure, ignoring alike the Golden Rule, the Sermon on the Mount, the divinely beautiful lesson of the Good Samaritan, and, in short, the more vital and central truth of the entire teaching of Jesus himself— the Fatherhood of God and the brotherhood of man."[2] Or, take another quotation from Professor Du Bois, which—whatever measure of truth or falsity there may be in it—has much more of

[1] "Souls of Black Folk," p. 43.
[2] "The Aftermath of Slavery," p. 4.

bitterness. Speaking of slavery, he says: "So after
the war, and even to this day, the religious and
ethical life of the South bows beneath this burden. Shrinking from facing the burning ethical
questions that front it unrelentingly, the Southern
Church clings all the more tenaciously to the letter of a wornout orthodoxy, while its inner,
truer soul crouches before and fears to answer
the problem of eight million black neighbors. It
therefore assiduously 'preaches Christ crucified'
in prayer meeting patois, and crucifies 'niggers'
in unrelenting daily life."[1] Such wholesale and
bitter denunciations of a whole people can be
nothing else than the expression of prejudice
rather than the word of statesmanship.

Northern Enthusiast

The third disturbing element is that of the
Northern enthusiast who feels sure he could
settle the whole race question if he had a few
years to give to it. It is a source of real rejoic-
ing to most men who earnestly face this question
that this tribe is rapidly dying out. Were it not
for these disturbing elements, the relations between the races would be cordial enough. It is
gratifying to note that in spite of them Dr.
Booker T. Washington, after an extended tour
through South Carolina, can say:

Booker T. Washington's Testimony

"My object in going on this educational tour
was to see for myself the actual condition of my
own race, and to say a word wherever I could

---

[1] "The Negro in the South," p. 170.

that would improve their life, and to note the actual relations existing between white people and black people, and to make a suggestion wherever I could that would further promote friendly relations. Of course, in a great State like South Carolina one cannot fail to see many things that are wrong, that are unjust, that need changing for the better. Notwithstanding this fact, I was surprised from the beginning to the end of the trip at the tremendous progress that the negro race is making, and at the friendly relations existing between black people and white people.

"In South Carolina, as in most parts of the South, I found the individual relations between black and white nearly all that could be hoped for. We frequently get a wrong impression of conditions in the South because we place too much dependence upon utterances made in Congress or in newspapers, or when some one is on parade. Everywhere I went I found at least one white man who believed implicitly in one negro; I found at least one negro who believed implicitly in one white man; and so it goes all through the South. So long as these individual relations are as kindly as they are, there is great hope for the future."[1]

The fact remains, however, that there is no small amount of unrest and race prejudice, which it behooves every sane searcher for truth and every true lover of his Southland to allay where possible. This can only be done after a careful and fair minded study of the whole race problem.

[1] *Outlook*, May 1, 1909.

Rightly Directed Progress

There is also need for study of this problem in order that the future advancement of the negro may be in the right direction. If we look to the single department of education, we must be convinced that the negro is advancing and will continue to advance whether we like it or not. If we of the South do not help direct this growing intellectual life, they of the North will, and we shall have no one but ourselves to blame if the education is falsely directed. Any one who fairly investigates the history of Northern philanthropy must be struck with the large unselfishness of the givers, even if their zeal does sometimes seem to act without sufficient knowledge. Much of this money has been poorly administered because we as Southern men, who ought to have been in position to give sane counsel, have not sufficiently studied this question to be able to formulate any reasonable constructive policy. After his tour through South Carolina to which I have referred, Booker T. Washington wrote to the *Outlook:*

"I was convinced, too, as I made this trip through the State of South Carolina, that more and more in the future an effort should be made to speak directly to the best type of Southern white people about our methods and aims in the education of the negro. There is too much discussion at long distance. In many cases the white people in the South do not understand the methods that are being pursued, nor the object sought. In proportion as we are perfectly frank with each other the difficulties are going to disappear, and larger amounts of money are going to be forthcoming from the South itself for the education of the black man."

There is further need of a constructive educational policy for the negro, because for every dollar given by Northern philanthropy, we ourselves have paid out of our own pockets probably ten dollars in taxes toward the negro public school. Up to 1906 it was estimated by the United States Commissioner of Education that for this purpose alone the South had paid $132,000,000 since the war. Mr. W. T. B. Williams, Field Agent of the Slater Fund, writing in the "Southern Workman," Nov., 1908, estimates the amount spent on negro public schools since 1870 at $155,000,000. During this period the illiteracy of the negro has been reduced by half. The negro is therefore being educated, however slowly. But how is he being educated? Is his increasing knowledge such as fits him for larger and better usefulness and for more worthy citizenship? Is he being educated away from life or into a truer life? These are the pertinent questions which every educated man of to-day must help to answer. Up to the present time, be it said to our shame, we have done little as Southern white men to answer these questions properly. It is no more than truth to say that General Armstrong, a Northern white man and a Union soldier, the founder of Hampton Institute, and Booker T. Washington, a Southern negro and an ex-slave, the founder of Tuskegee, have probably done more than any dozen Southern white men to answer these questions aright.

We need more Southern men who can write and speak with the knowledge and sanity of Edgar Gardner Murphy, in his "The Present South" if we are to give proper direction to this new intellectual movement.

Encouragement

Again, we should study this question in order that we may know the encouragement of the negro's progress. Not a few Southern men have become darkly pessimistic about the future of the negro race. Some think that the door of hope is forever shut in his face. I must confess that, although a Southern man, reared in the midst of the large negro population of Texas, and attending college in Nashville, a city where negro education is at its best, I have been constantly surprised at the marvellous progress of the negro race. In 1908, Ray Stannard Baker estimated that negroes owned 1,400,000 acres of land in the State of Georgia alone, and paid taxes on $28,000,000 worth of property. Prof. John W. Gilbert, one of the most capable and sane negro leaders in the South, has recently estimated that negroes own 200,000 farms, worth approximately $700,000,000, and that $500,000,000 worth of these farms are entirely free of debt; that in 1900, in cities and villages, negroes owned 126,329 homes free from debt; and that negroes—not stinting in their contributions—have built churches valued at $40,-000,000. Forty-eight per cent. of the race are members of churches, and the generous contributions they make annually to missions would put

to shame many of our wealthy white churches.
Booker T. Washington has said, again and
again, that fifty-seven per cent. of the negro race
is now literate, although forty years ago illiteracy
was well-nigh universal.

But these figures are abstract, and the real
story of race progress is only thoroughly
understood when one goes into the best barber shop in Atlanta and finds it owned and
operated by a negro, with negro barbers
at the chairs, or visits a Georgia plantation
of a thousand acres—as it is possible to do—
owned by one negro, or goes into the home of an
educated negro, as I did recently in Texas—
where the building is commodious and modern,
where there are good carpets on the floors, a piano
in the parlor, and you could not tell from appear-
ances that a white banker did not live there. Or,
if one wants further to be convinced of this
progress, let him visit a high-grade negro church.
Some months ago one of the connectional officers
of the Methodist Episcopal Church South and I
had to break our journey across the South by
stopping in a Southern city to spend Sunday. At
eleven o'clock we went up to the first church and
listened to a good average sermon from the
pastor. After the service we went for a walk
before dinner and chanced to come upon a leading negro church. We went in, and found the
first floor filled to overflowing with a well-
dressed, orderly and reverent congregation—it
would seem more than a thousand—so we were
shown to the gallery by a polite and altogether
well-appearing negro. The sermon had just

begun from the text: "I am the way, the truth and the life." It was clear, logical, filled with practical and helpful truth, and as it progressed my connectional officer and preacher friend leaned over and whispered to me: "The white church would do mighty well to trade preachers with this negro church." And he was perfectly right. The whole service was of a high order, and would have done grace to any white church I ever attended.

Tuskegee

Or, if one prefers, let him visit Tuskegee, and look into the faces of fourteen hundred negro boys and girls; hear their trained chorus of a hundred voices render the old plantation melodies with matchless power; go to their wood shops, blacksmith shops, model laundry, bakery, millinery establishment, and see the splendid work done; hold a Bible study institute for five hours on a hot spring day without anybody leaving; see five hundred and twenty-five men enroll in the voluntary study of the Bible; and three years later learn that the number has grown to seven hundred and thirty; finally, let him learn that not a single graduate of this school has ever been in jail for any crime whatsoever—and if he does not have some hope for the negro and believe he is making substantial progress, he would be hard to convince.

Physical Needs

Lastly, we should study the problem for the sake of the help it will enable us to render a

backward race in its hour of need. These needs
are, first of all, physical. So long as millions of
these people live in the one-roomed cabin, which
is poorly ventilated, poorly heated, and not
lighted at all; so long as millions more live in
the crowded tenement section or in the damp
alleys of our cities in houses that have neither
sanitation nor comfort; so long as the bath tub is
almost an unknown luxury in the great mass of
negro homes; so long as four, five, or even ten
negroes are sleeping in one crowded little tenement room; so long as the death rate of negroes
is from eight to twelve more per thousand than
that for white people; so long as deaths from
venereal diseases among colored people are six to
seven times as great as among white people—if
the Alabama statistics for certain periods can be
trusted—and so long as the negro mortality from
consumption in many of our leading cities is from
fifty to one hundred and fifty per cent. in advance
of the corresponding white mortality—just so
long will the Southern white man have an obligation to study these facts, find their causes, and
apply cures.

Intellectual Needs

The next great need of the negro is training.
While marvellous progress has been made, forty-
three per cent. of this race is illiterate. Even
if $155,000,000 has been spent on public
schools for negroes since 1870, the average length
of school term has never been and is not now over
seventy days per year[1] According to the report

---

[1] School reports for the present year make a much
better showing than this.

of the Superintendent of Colored Normal Schools in North Carolina for the year 1908, the average cost of public school buildings used for negro schools was $124.37. Out of 2,198 such buildings, only 64 had patent desks—all the others being furnished with simple benches. This makes any genuine school work next to impossible. In thirty counties in this State, the country school teachers were paid less than seventeen dollars per month on the average, and in these counties there were 59,665 negro children of school age, and yet it is a known fact that, in proportion to her wealth, North Carolina is spending more than almost any other State in the Union on the education of her youth. Surely the knowledge of such facts should impel us to do more for general education. In addition, there is the greatest need of industrial and mechanical education. According to a computation of Thomas Jesse Jones in the "Southern Workman," March, 1909, the product per agricultural worker in 1900 was for the State of Iowa, $1,088; for New Hampshire, $477; Alabama, $150.98; North Carolina, $149.75; South Carolina, $147.46, or the Iowa worker, largely because of greater skill, is able to produce more than seven times as much wealth annually as the worker in South Carolina. We in the South cannot afford to allow this disparity of wealth producing ability to continue. There are at present a few thousand students in industrial schools like Tuskegee and Hampton Institute, but the number ought to be multiplied ten-fold. Who will see that this is done if we of the South remain ignorant of our great in-

dustrial need? Why leave this mass of humanity
in a half-fed and half-starved condition? Why
not train their hands and their heads so that they
may not only secure competence for themselves,
but add millions annually to the wealth of the
section. What we need more than any other one
element in our Southern industrial life is trained
laborers. There are eight million negroes in our
very midst; the graduates of Hampton and Tuskegee have forever dispelled the doubt that
they can be made efficient workmen by proper
training; when will there be enough of constructive study and statesmanship in the South to
harness this mighty force and make it the wonder
of the world in its wealth producing power?

As Mr. Murphy has put it: "The only real peril
of our situation is, not in any aspect of the
negro's wise and legitimate progress, but rather
in the danger that the negro will know so little,
will do so little, and will increasingly care so
little about knowing and doing, that the great
black mass of his numbers, his ignorance, his idle-
ness, and his lethargy will drag forever like a
cancerous and suffocating burden at the heart of
our Southern life,"[1]

Moral Needs

Lastly, one must mention the moral needs of
the negro. While forty-eight per cent. of the
whole colored population of the South has a
church affiliation, and while $40,000,000 have
been invested in churches, there is nevertheless a
terrible moral corruption that eats at the vitals

---

[1] "The Present South," p. 61.

of the negro race. A Christian negro physician told me recently that ninety-eight per cent. was a low estimate for the negro men who have been socially impure. Cheap whiskey and cocaine are doing their deadly work for literally thousands of negro men and women. Profanity, gambling and debauchery are everywhere prevalent. All of these vices are destroying the body and damning the souls of countless thousands. Add to this the fact that in the rural churches the religion is all too frequently of an emotional type, which is completely divorced from ethical action, and the further fact that not infrequently the minister is himself leprous with the sins of laziness, dishonesty and impurity and the picture darkens until one is most sick at heart.

What shall we do about such crying needs as these? Shall we close our eyes and remain in blissful ignorance? Shall we waive the whole matter aside and say that the race is unworthy of our attention and effort? Or shall we fairly face these problems and do our part in bringing to them a real solution? It is always easier to close one's eyes to the hard and unpleasant things of life—but is it always manly? No man has ever been a prophet to humanitywho has not faced the facts, however unpleasant. He who is not willing to bear the heartache of knowing the world's sorrow and suffering and sin can never know the joy of being a messenger of a new and brighter day. One is profoundly sorry for that sweet girl graduate who went home with her diploma in her hand after hearing a commencement address on the struggle of men, and, throwing herself into a chair, said: "Oh, mother, I wish people wouldn't talk so much about the struggles and hardships of the masses—it makes one so uncomfortable."

The White Man's Obligation

It is just because the negro is ignorant; just because he is having a hard battle to win industrial competence; just because he is sinking under the burdens of awful diseases; and just because he has not yet attained unto the full stature of moral manhood that every college man is under obligation to know and better his condition. It is because we of the South love our homes and want to protect them, that we must no longer remain ignorant of this question. It is because we are born in a section immortalized by such spirits as Lee and Jackson, who gave their lives for its welfare, that we, in this hour of our Southland's greatest need, will not prove traitors, but will, with the hearts of true sons, bring to its aid the largest knowledge, the sanest judgment, the clearest thought which loyal sons can bring.

II

THE ECONOMIC CONDITION OF THE NEGRO

SLOW THROUGH THE DARK

Slow moves the pageant of a climbing race;
  Their footsteps drag far, far below the height,
  And, unprevailing by their utmost might,
Seems faltering downward from each won place.
No strange, swift-sprung exception we; we trace
  A devious way thro' dim, uncertain light—
  Our hope, through the long-vistaed years, a sight
Of that our Captain's soul sees face to face.
  Who, faithless, faltering that the road is steep,
Now raiseth up his drear insistent cry?
  Who stoppeth here to spend a while in sleep,
Or curses that the storm obscures the sky?
  Heed not the darkness round you, dull and deep;
The clouds grown thickest when the summit's high.

—PAUL LAURENCE DUNBAR.

II

THE ECONOMIC CONDITION OF THE NEGRO

One can scarcely hope to understand the economic life of the American negro without at least a brief glance at the economic conditions in Africa, his native home. Most of the American slaves were brought from that section of Africa extending from the Congo region to the northward and around the Gulf of Guinea. They were largely taken from the Bantus and the Nigritians occupying this territory. This is the most fertile section of Africa—if we exclude the Nile Valley—including a large part of the banana zone, where the native lives upon the bounties of nature almost without labor. The banana and plantain grow in abundance and fish and game are easily secured. No man needs to lie awake at night wondering from whence his next day's provisions will come. They are all about him and will almost fall into his hands without the effort to reach forth for them.

Little Division of Labor in Africa

There is very little division of labor in this section, for there are no trades, though a little blacksmithing, pottery making, dyeing, basket weaving, cattle raising, poultrying, etc., are carried on. Most of the work is done by the

women. Where there is need of more laborers,
the men, rather than work themselves, have from
time immemorial enslaved their neighbors; so
that slavery is native to Africa and is not in any
sense an institution introduced into African life
by the white man. The ancestry of the American negro having been surrounded by such conditions, it is hardly accurate to apply the term
"economic" to the earlier stages of his development.

Negro Needed to Learn to Work

When the negro came to America the greatest need he had was to learn to work. It is the
recognition of this fact that has led not a few
people into the error of thinking that slavery was
an unmixed blessing to the negro. As an institution, it cannot be said to have been a blessing,
though out of it did come some rich blessings to
the slave. It is necessary to see what slavery did
for the negro before we can fully appreciate his
present economic life. Lest I be misunderstood,
I wish to let Principal Booker T. Washington
speak to this point: "The climatic and other new
conditions required that the slave should wear
clothing, a thing, for the most part, new to him.
. . . The economic element not only made it
necessary that the negro slave should be clothed
for the sake of decency and in order to preserve
his health, but the same considerations made it
necessary that he should be housed and taught
the comforts to be found in a home. Within
a few months, then, after the arrival of the negro
in America, he was wearing clothes and liv-

ing in a house—no inconsiderable step in the direction of morality and Christianity. . . . There is another important element. In his native country, owing to climatic conditions, and also because of his few simple and crude wants, the negro before coming to America had little necessity to labor. . . . Notwithstanding the fact that in most cases the element of compulsion entered into the labor of the slave, and the main object sought was the enrichment of the owner, the American negro had, under the régime of slavery, his first lesson, in anything like continuous, progressive systematic labor. I have said that two of the signs of Christianity are clothes and houses, and now I add a third, "work".[1]

Influence of Labor on Character

The necessity of continued and systematic labor is one of the hardest lessons which humanity has had to learn, but it is just in proportion as this lesson is learned that civilization has progressed. If one goes into Africa to-day and starts northward from the Equator he will pass successively through the banana zone, the grain zone, the cattle zone and the desert or camel zone. In the first, the native does not have to labor for food, and civilization is at an extremely low ebb. Prof. Dowd has said of these vegetarian negroes that they are the most brutal people in the world. Moral life here is very low, and political organization almost unknown, save among the Ashantis and the Dahomans. As one moves northward into the second section mentioned,

[1] "The Negro in the South," pp. 18-21 passim.

the grain zone, he discovers that fruit is less abundant, nature more niggardly, and that, consequently, man must begin to labor to sustain life. A marked improvement is seen here in the moral, social, and intellectual conditions. When one goes still further, into the cattle-raising zone, where still more of vigilance and labor must be bestowed on the flocks and herds, he notices that the advancement in civilization is even more marked. Labor seems to bring out the best qualities of human nature; it seems to give stability and strength to character. No nation or individual can hope to build real character where labor is despised. Perhaps this is one reason for the frequent degeneration of the idle rich.

If, then, slavery did teach the negro the lesson of systematic labor, Principal Washington is surely right in maintaining that this lesson was one of the first steps in the life of the negro toward civilization, morality, and Christianity.

Early Slaves Were Unskilled Laborers

The work of the slave was always, on the whole, heavy labor, in distinction from skilled labor; and this was peculiarly true when he first landed in America. He was then entirely untrained and fitted only for the crudest and simplest forms of work. But as years went by, these people began to get that training which fitted them to become the skilled laborers of the South. The large plantation system was most favorable to such training. Every plantation was a little world within itself, where practically every article of consumption was hand-made. Hence it came about that most of the larger plantations had slaves trained to be blacksmiths, carpenters, shoemakers, wheelwrights, seamstresses, expert cooks, etc. In this way thousands of negroes received a practical and efficient technical education, which they have sadly missed since slavery days. Dr. Washington in speaking of this phase of slavery says: "I do not overstate the matter when I say that I am quite sure that in one county in the South during the days of slavery there were more colored youths being taught trades than there are members of my race now being taught trades in any of the larger cities of the North".[1]

Skilled Laborers Among Slaves

The result of all this was that, at the opening of the Civil War, the negroes of the South had wellnigh a monopoly of all the forms of mechanical and skilled labor. One who learned his trade under a slave artisan writes as follows:[2] "One needs only to go down South and examine hundreds of old Southern mansions and splendid old church edifices, still intact, to be convinced of the fact of the cleverness of the negro artisan who constructed nine-tenths of them, and many of them still provoke the admiration of all who see them, and are not to be despised by the men of our day. . . . Much has been said of the new negro for the new century, but with all his training he will have to take a long

---

[1] "The Negro in the South," p. 24.
[2] "The Negro Artisan," pp. 16 and 19.

stride in mechanical skill before he reaches the point of practical efficiency where the old negro of the old century left off."

Labor Considered Degrading

But it must be remembered that slavery had another side in relation to the economic training of the negro. While it did train him to work, it nevertheless taught him to connect all labor with the condition of slavery. It was inevitable that he should feel that labor was degrading, since he saw the slave owners keeping free from manual toil. The outcome was natural—that when he attained freedom he turned his back on all manual labor. The race has not yet been able to overcome this false conception, and it is not to be required that it should have done so in two generations. Those of us who are disposed to condemn the negro in a wholesale manner, for his laziness and unwillingness to work systematically, need to remember the time in our own childhood when labor was a nightmare, though we would readily have done the same things had they been called play. It was the word "work" that annoyed and bullied us; one needs only to know boys to-day to see the dread inspired by that word.

This aversion to work because it was a slave's part, and the firm belief that the national government planned to care for and feed the newly emancipated slave, sent thousands of them from the farms and plantations, at the close of the war to wander aimlessly about seeking a living, but unwilling to labor for the same.

Negro Overcoming Aversion to Work

Little by little the negro is overcoming this aversion to manual toil. This fact is clearly proved by the new attitude toward industrial education. When it was first started in Hampton Institute by General Armstrong, the race as a whole—in so far as it knew of this type of training—rose up in arms against it. Dr. Washington has said again and again that he met the bitterest opposition from parents when he inaugurated his work at Tuskegee. These parents protested that they had worked all their lives and they wanted their children trained in the "Books." "I remember that for a number of years after the founding of the Tuskegee Institute, objection on the part of parents and on the part of students poured in upon me from day to day. The parents said that they wanted their children taught "the book," but they did not want them taught anything concerning farming or household duties. It was curious to note how most of the people worshiped "the book." The parent did not care what was inside the book; the harder and longer the name of it, the better it satisfied the parent every time; and the more books you could require the child to purchase, the better teacher you were. His reputation as a first-class pedagogue was added to very largely in that section if the teacher required the child to buy a long string of books each year and each month. I found some white people who had the same idea. . . . From Hampton and Tuskegee and other large educational centres the idea of industrial education has spread

throughout the South, and there are now scores
of institutions that are giving this kind of training in a most effective and helpful manner; so
that, in my opinion, the greatest thing we have
accomplished for the negro race within the last
twenty-five years has been to rid his mind of
all idea of labor's being degrading. This has
been no inconsiderable achievement. If I were
asked to point out the greatest change accomplished for the negro race, I would say that it
was not a tangible, physical change, but a change
of the spirit—the new idea of our people with
respect to negro labor." [1]

House Servants Not Yet Very Reliable

This change of ideals and spirit is less marked
in some classes of negroes than in others.
In the lower classes, where the wants are few
and where the standards of living are very low,
labor is avoided just as much as possible. If
three days' wages will support an individual
for the week, then three days' labor per
week is about all that can be got out of that individual. Many of the housekeepers of the
South have become utterly discouraged with and
have lost faith in the race, because the least rain
or an especially cold wave or hot weather—in
fact almost anything in the way of a change—
serves as a pretext to keep their cooks and housemaids away from their duties. So marvelous is
the number of "grandmothers" and "uncles" and
"aunts" some maids lose by death—and they of
course, must attend the funeral and lose at least

---

[1] "The Negro in the South," p. 48 and p. 50.

two days of work—one begins to feel that some of the house servants must be first-cousins to every negro in the city.

Southern White Women Pessimistic

In view of the unsatisfactory nature of house servants, it is not strange that the women of the South are often inclined to take a much more gloomy view of the future of the negro than are the men. But I should not be fair if I did not say here that very few Southern white women ever know or have any contact whatever with the better class of negroes or even with the middle class. The house servants as a whole belong to the lowest strata of negro life; they have had less training and are more lacking in ambition than any other class. The demand is so large that they can get work at almost any hour; therefore they feel practically independent.

The present situation is not altogether the fault of this type of negro. He has no training. He has not been taught to take a pride in his work. He has failed to develop any real desire for comforts at home. It is not at all strange that he should be immoral, lazy and untrustworthy. It ought to be said also that far too little care is often exercised to train the servants in our homes. We show too little interest in them. We have never seen the inside of their homes. We have never done anything to make their home lives a little more bearable. We have taken no interest in them outside of what they do for us, and consequently they take no interest in us outside of what they

can get from us. It is not far from a game of
"tit for tat."

Possibilities of Better House Servants

That even this type of negro is capable of
faithfulness and systematic labor can be proved
by unnumbered cases of the servant class. I
know many homes where the cook or housemaid has given continuous service for five, ten
or fifteen years. We have in my own home a
faithful old cook who was trained up under the
slave régime; and although she is getting old
now, she is as conscientious, as punctual, as efficient in her service as one could possibly ask
any servant to be. This woman had splendid
training in her girlhood and she has never got
away from it. She not only knows how, but
she is willing and glad to work. What we need
at present in the South is a little more care in
the training of house servants. Thousands of
Southern white women take a genuine interest
in their servants, visit them when they are sick,
try to improve their home life, and endeavor
in every way possible to elevate them and make
them more efficient, just as the best mistresses did
in slave days. But there are many others who
take no such interest. We ourselves must continue to suffer the consequences of servants
poorly trained and lacking in a sense of responsibility. When all the women in the South take
a genuine interest in the negro women and girls
in their homes there will be the dawning of a new
day in the condition of the servant.

The South's Debt of Gratitude to the Negro

One need not stop here to lay emphasis on the large part which the slave had in the building of the economic life of the South before the War. To the negro the South owes a debt of real gratitude for its rapid agricultural growth; and in no less degree does every true son of the South owe the negro a debt of gratitude for his unselfishness, his faithfulness, and his devotion to the whites of the section during the dark and bloody days of the Civil War. Looking back on that period from the present unrest, one marvels that, during all those days of civil strife, no planter ever had the least fear in leaving his wife and daughters in the care of the trusted slave. So far as I have been able to learn, not a single slave ever betrayed that sacred trust.

Present Conditions—The Farmer

We must turn now and ask, What can be seen in the present life of the negro as the effect of the long apprenticeship in slavery? Looking first at the negro farmer, one is not altogether encouraged. One can hardly read a sadder story than that told in such beautiful English by Professor Du Bois in his "Souls of Black Folk." Here he pictures the negro farmer in Dougherty County, Georgia. Poor, shiftless, living in broken-down houses, tilling the barren and unproductive soil, with worthless stock for which he has paid double prices, and carrying always a load of debt which enslaves him to the storekeeper. The old slave owner moved away after the War because the land was too poor to support him, and his land was rented to the poor whites. Later, the poor whites found the cultivation of this land unprofitable; so, they moved out and left the negro to eke out his meagre living from the impoverished soil. This is all too true a picture of a large part of South Carolina and of other sections of the South. The blight of all these poorer sections of the South has been the wasteful and unscientific methods of farming. Nor is one much more encouraged when he studies the conditions of the negro farm tenant in the richer land sections of Mississippi, Louisiana, and Arkansas. Here the large plantations still retain much of the nature of the old slave régime, with its negro quarters, its broad acreage, etc. There is one striking contrast— the wholesale moving of the tenants at the end of the year. Here the negro must be fed from the proprietor's commissary, just as the slaves were formerly fed from the master's "smoke house." At the end of the year the negro not infrequently finds his account at the commissary to be larger than the assets from his crop, with the result that he is still a slave, though now his bondage is not legal but economic.

Mr. Stone's Experiments

Perhaps the best picture of the dark side of this type of tenantry is drawn by Mr. Stone in his "Studies in the American Race Problem." After discussing some discouraging experiments which he himself tried in Mississippi, he goes on to give an account of cotton raising by Italian laborers in the state of Arkansas. The comparison with negro labor is not very favorable.

"The number of Italian squads in 1898 was 38, with 200 working hands, cultivating 1,200 acres of cotton. Of negro squads there were 203, with 600 working hands, cultivating 2,600 acres of cotton. At the end of 1905, after eight years, there were on the property 107 Italian squads, with 500 working hands, and 38 negro families, with 175 working hands—an increase of 69 squads and 300 hands for the Italians, a decrease of 105 squads and 425 hands for the negro. The total cotton acreage has increased to 3,900, of which the Italians are cultivating 3,000 acres and the negroes 900. This bare statement of numerical loss and gain is of itself pregnant with meaning.

"This gives us the following results: Average number of squads Italians 52, negroes 167, average number of working hands, Italians 269 negroes 433; average number of acres per working hand, Italians, 6.2, negroes 5.1; average pounds of lint per hand, Italians 2,584, negroes 1,174; average pounds of lint per acre, Italians 403, negroes 233; average cash product value per hand (cotton and seed), Italians $277.36, negroes $128.47; average cash product value per acre, Italians $44.77, negroes $26.36. Thus the Italian is seen to have produced more lint per hand, by 1,410 pounds, or 120.1 per cent, and to have exceeded the negro yield per acre by 170 pounds or 72.9 per cent. The difference in money value in favor of the Italian was $148.89

per hand, or 115.8 per cent, and $18.41 per acre,
or 69.8 per cent.

"To state it bluntly and coldly, it is for the
negro a recital of conditions as old as his freedom: too much time spent out of his crop and
away from his work; too much waiting for the
weather to improve; too much putting off to a
more convenient season; a too constant and too
successful besieging of those in authority for
money accommodations and supplies; too little
reckoning against the future day of settlement;
too much "leaning on the Lord," and too little
upon himself, in things not spiritual; too much
living for to-day and not enough for to-morrow." [1]

The thing which vitiates Mr. Stone's conclusions is perhaps lack of perspective. He is just
a little too closely associated with the problem.
He himself owns and operates a large plantation in Mississippi, and is a little apt to be prejudiced by the success or failure of his own isolated experiments. Mr. Stone's full and valuable
statements concerning the supplanting of negro
plantation hands by Italians and other foreigners
does not seem to me to prove anything, save that
the negro is inefficient and that, consequently,
the whole South is suffering from his lack of
economic efficiency. It does not at all answer
the question of how we can get more efficient
laborers to supplant him. The truth is, most
men who have carefully studied the question have
deliberately concluded that the negro farm hand

---

[1] Stone—"Studies in the American Race Problem,"
pp. 182, 183, 184.

will not be supplanted to any large extent by white immigrants, however desirable such an exchange may or may not be. Farming in the South is now largely a question of holding the negro laborer in the country and making him efficient.

Encouraging Features of Negro Farm Life

There is, however, a brighter side to this question of the negro farmer. First of all, the negro is slowly but surely becoming the tiller of his own land. Dr. Booker T. Washington said in his annual address at the National Negro Business League in nineteen hundred and ten: "Perhaps never before have the negroes added to their wealth so rapidly as they are adding at present. The negroes of Georgia during the present year added 47,045 acres to their land holdings, and increased the value of their land holdings $636,532. . . . The negroes of Virginia also during the year 1909 added 53,452 acres to their land holdings and increased their land values by $175,740."[1] While it cannot be said that there is any hope that the majority of negro farmers will own their land within the next two generations, it nevertheless does keep one from despairing of the future to learn that such substantial progress as these figures indicate is being made.

Better Methods of Farming

There is a second note of encouragement about the negro farmer. He is learning to farm with

[1] Report of Eleventh Annual Convention Nat. Negro Bus. League, p. 82.

more intelligence than formerly. He is building
up his land, rotating his crops, diversifying his
products, and, on the whole, making genuine
progress. The farmers' institutes at Tuskegee
and Hampton, together with the wide publicity
given through the negro press to their proceed-
ings, have had much to do with this marked improvement. The agricultural demonstration
trains in the South have been another factor in
this development. The agricultural colleges and
the agricultural training in the public schools,
though very inefficient as yet, have had their
share in bringing about better farming methods.
Lastly, the negro demonstration agents of the
Agricultural Department of the United States
Government have had no small share in these
improved methods. "Eight of the graduates (of
the Agricultural Department at Tuskegee) are
working for the United States Department
of Agriculture as Agricultural Demonstration
Agents, in the states of Alabama, Louisiana,
Mississippi, Oklahoma, South Carolina, and Virginia. The purpose of the Demonstration Work
is to get a farmer in a community to set aside a
small portion of his land and to plant and culti-
vate it under the direction of a Government expert. Other farmers in the community are invited to come and see how the selected plot is
prepared, planted and cultivated. They are induced to put into practice what they have learned.
Thus by means of a single tract of land, the
farming methods of an entire community are improved, and the yield of products greatly increased. Where farmers formerly raised 5 to 15

bushels of corn per acre, they are now, because of the teaching of these Demonstration Agents, raising from 30 to 60 bushels. Where from 150 to 200 pounds of lint cotton were produced per acre, now from 250 to 600 pounds are being produced per acre.

"The Demonstration Agents do not confine themselves to teaching improved farming methods, but they also assist the people in getting better live stock, having better gardens and improving their homes." [1]

Turning from the economic conditions of the farmers to that of the artisans, we at once face serious problems. When the Civil War closed, although the negro was the skilled laborer, he had many serious handicaps. First of all, he had never been in the habit of making independent contracts, but had always worked under white contractors. As a slave, he had had his owner to stand responsible for him, acting as his bond, as it were. But now that freedom had come, and with it the bitter feeling arising out of Reconstruction days, it was not always easy for the negro artisan to find a white man who would act as bondsman, though many of the old masters did so with their own ex-slaves. Nor was it always easy for the artisan to secure work.

Artisans' Need of Scientific Training

Then the negro artisan, although a very admirable workman for the cruder forms of mechanical work on a plantation, had too little edu-

---

[1] "Industrial Work of Tuskegee Graduates," p. 6.

cation to take hold readily of the rapidly
developing complications in the mechanical
world. He was sadly in need of technical training to enable him to understand and handle
quickly new tools and new machinery. Lastly,
there was the handicap to which we have referred
earlier—the conception that labor was degrading. With all these drawbacks, it is not strange
that the negro rapidly lost a part of his prestige
as a skilled workman.

Shut Out by Labor Unions

At the present time, a serious handicap of the
negro artisan is the labor union. In the North
the negro is usually excluded from unions and
effectually debarred from all skilled labor. In
that section there is practically no avenue of ac-
tivity open to him save that of the servant. "The
Negro Artisan," a study made under the direction of Atlanta University, says: "Nine-tenths
of the black membership of the carpenters is in
the South and mostly organized in separate
unions from the whites. In the North, there
are very few in the unions; there are a few in
the West. In great cities like Washington,
Baltimore, Cincinnati, Philadelphia, New York,
and even Boston, it is almost impossible for a
negro to be admitted to the unions, and there is
no appeal from the decision." [1]

This same publication, after a most exhaustive
study, gives the following estimation of the attitude of the unions toward the negro in fifteen
forms of skilled employment:

---

[1] "The Negro Artisan," p. 160.

"Miners—Welcome negroes in nearly all cases.

Longshoremen—Welcome negroes in nearly all cases.

Cigarmakers—Admit practically all applicants.

Barbers—Admit many, but restrain negroes when possible.

Seamen—Admit many, but prefer whites.

Firemen—Admit many, but prefer whites.

Tobacco workers—Admit many, but prefer whites.

Carriage and wagon workers—Admit some, but do not seek negroes.

Brickmakers—Admit some, but do not seek negroes.

Coopers—Admit some, but do not seek negroes.

Broommakers—Admit some, but do not seek negroes.

Plasterers—Admit freely in South and a few in North.

Carpenters—Admit many in South, almost none in North.

Masons—Admit many in South, almost none in North.

Painters—Admit a few in South, almost none in North." [1]

---

[1] "The Negro Artisan," p. 163.

Southern Situation—Unequal Wages

Turning from the North to the South, we find a very different situation. Here the labor unions have much less hold; and even where these are strong, negroes are either admitted into the general union or have separate organizations. The main handicap in this section is not that the negro is shut out from the skilled professions, but that he is paid from ten to fifteen per cent less than the white man, on the average, for similar services. Whether this lower wage is due to lack of efficiency or to race distinctions would be very hard to determine. The careful study of the Atlanta University made in 1902 seems to indicate that the negro artisan in the South is just about holding his own, or perhaps losing his hold in a small degree. This conclusion is confirmed by Dr. Booker T. Washington in the following terms: "It has seemed to many persons that the negro, in losing his monopoly in the trades, was losing also his position in them. After a careful study of the facts, I have come to the conclusion that this is not true. What the facts do seem to show is that there is in process a re-distribution of the colored population among the different trades and professions. There were fewer negroes engaged in farm labor in 1900, for instance, but there is a larger proportion of the negro population engaged in the other four general classes of labor than there was in 1890." [1]

Dr. Washington gives the following table, in-

---

[1] "The Story of the Negro," Vol. II, p. 66.

dicating the increase of negroes employed in the main classes of occupation:

	1890	1900
" Agricultural pursuits ..	1,984,310	2,143,176
Professional service ...	33,994	47,324
Domestic and personal service	956,754	1,324,160
Trade and transportation	145,717	209,154
Manufacturing and mechanical pursuits	208,374	275,149"[1]

All the reliable evidence that I have been able to obtain indicates that the negro in the South has lost, or is losing, his monopoly of certain trades, but is at the same time entering new trades, thus very nearly if not quite, holding his own in the skilled occupations.

Influence of Industrial Training

Perhaps it ought to be said here that one of the influences that has helped the negro to hold his own in the trades is the new industrial training. Hampton and Tuskegee, with their many smaller but worthy followers, have been sending out large numbers of skilled laborers, who have become leaders in their professions. During the twenty-nine years of its existence, Tuskegee alone has sent out nine thousand students, each of whom has had two years of careful industrial training. The average cost per year for the training of each of these students has been $81.50. Principal Washington estimates from carefully collected data that the average prop-

---

[1] "The Story of the Negro," Vol. II, p. 67

erty holdings of these nine thousand students is $1,700 each. If this be anything like a true estimate, surely industrial training is a paying proposition for the South.

Twenty-three industrial schools have been established by Tuskegee graduates and perhaps an equal number by graduates of Hampton. In this manner, the idea of the dignity of labor is being brought home to the masses, and thousands of boys and girls are being fitted for industrial efficiency. Further discussion of industrial training must be left for a following chapter.

The Negro in Business

There has been witnessed during the last few years a very marvelous development of business interests among negroes in the South. One could hardly illustrate the diversity of business interests better than by giving a list of negro activities in one Southern city: "We can perhaps best realize these conditions by picturing a single community: Jacksonville, Florida, for instance, had 16,000 negroes in 1900. To-day it has nine colored lawyers, eighteen colored physicians, ten drug stores, two sanitariums, one bank, one livery, sale and feed stable, two garages, ten real estate dealers, three undertaking establishments, three denominational schools and a school for girls only, one old folks' home, one orphanage, one industrial school, one institutional church which operates a sewing class, dressmaking, bookkeeping, kindergarten, cooking, gymnasium, music—instrumental and vocal;

has two paid missionaries, an assistant pastor. The church owns a full city block in the heart of the city, valued at $125,000. There are two dentists, a colored board of trade, the first and only one in the South; three cigar factories, three wholesale fish and poultry dealers; four hotels, containing twenty-five to one hundred rooms each; three weekly newspapers; one Odd Fellows Temple, valued at $100,000, and one K. of P. Temple, both paid for; several Masonic Temples of less value; one large jewelry store; one curio store; ten public school buildings; twenty-six letter carriers and postal clerks; three deputy collectors of customs; numbers of railway mail clerks; one shoe store; two industrial insurance companies that own their buildings, one valued at $35,000." [1]

Varieties of Occupation

In going through the 1910 report of the National Negro Business League, I find the following business interests, trades and professions represented in the roster of delegates: Druggist, General Merchant, Undertaker, Banker, Coal Dealer, Haberdasher, Insurance and Real Estate Agent, Truck Farmer, Barber, Dealer in Dry Goods, Harness Maker, Mail Carrier, Teacher, Planter, Lawyer, Hotel and Restaurant Keeper, Chiropodist, Contractor, Poultry Raiser, Tinsmith, Shoe Dealer, Delicatessen Dealer, Publisher of Books and Newspapers, Expressman, Hair Dresser, Drug Manufacturer, Tan-

[1] " Social Betterment," Atlanta University publication, No. 14, p. 12.

ner, Miner, Veterinary Surgeon, Photographer, Brick Mason, Butcher, Stenographer, Tailor, Laundryman, Broker, Liveryman and Feed Merchant, Garage Keeper, Blacksmith, etc.

In the one line of banking, it is surprising to find that there are fifty-six banks now owned and operated by negroes. Ten of these are in the State of Mississippi alone. Another form of business which is growing very rapidly is industrial insurance. In the State of North Carolina, one industrial insurance company paid out, in 1909, $114,000 to its policy holders.

Negro Business Man's Opportunity in the South

The business opportunity of the negro in the South is practically unlimited. In the first place, there is a growing race pride among the negroes, and they are beginning to patronize increasingly their own dealers. There never has been any objection on the part of white people to patronizing negro business concerns, provided they furnished equal value for the money expended. Scott Bond, an ex-slave and negro merchant in Madison, Arkansas, said in his address to the American Negro Business League: "Both black and white patronize us and I want to say, to the credit of the Southern white man, the chance for a negro to succeed in the South, in a business way, is as good as it can possibly be anywhere." [1]

One Remarkably Successful Business

Perhaps I can best convey my own feeling of

[1] Report for 1910 of the "American Negro Business League," p. 92.

encouragement over the negro's economic efficiency in business by giving a brief account of a visit I made on Monday, January 2nd, 1911, to the plant of the National Baptist Publishing Board, 523 Second Avenue, North, Nashville, Tennessee. I reached the plant about half-past one in the afternoon and found everything quiet and all the operatives out save one old attendant, who said the annual dinner to the employees was being served by Dr. R. H. Boyd, the proprietor (a negro), in the adjoining chapel. On sending in my name, I was invited into the hall, where a liberal feast had evidently been provided, as was evidenced by the appearance of turkey bones left on the table. Of course, the advent of two white men called for speeches; so my friend and I made remarks and then had the chance of hearing ourselves outstripped by the flowery eloquence of some of the colored "brethren." Among others, Dr. Boyd himself gave a brief talk, outlining the growth of the business. He started his publishing business, he said, in 1896, with two "split bottom" chairs in a small room, with a "green negro girl" as his employed force. Brandon, Bush, and other white printers in the city did his printing by contract. This little one-roomed office had grown in fifteen years to a series of two-story brick buildings—all owned by Dr. Boyd—containing the most modern revolving presses and all the necessary printing appliances. The one "green negro girl" was now aided by one hundred and fifty negro employees, including everybody from the "printer's devil" up to the bookkeepers, stenographers, and an editor of religious articles, who was also chaplain of the factory.

A new department has now been added, where church furniture and stained glass are manufactured for negro churches, and also a doll department, where thousands of real negro dolls are sold all over the country to negro merchants. I went through all the buildings under Dr. Boyd's guidance and was impressed with the economy, the careful arrangement and marked efficiency of the whole plant. One detail I cannot forbear mentioning. Dr. Boyd told us that the chapel where the New Year's dinner was served each year—just as I had seen it that day —was built especially for religious services for the employed force. Every morning at nine o'clock every wheel in the factory is stopped and each employee goes to the chapel, where the chaplain conducts a half-hour service of Bible reading and study. No man or woman who will not attend chapel regularly can hold his position in the establishment. One of the white printers of Nashville once remonstrated with Dr. Boyd for wasting half an hour each day from the time of so many laborers. The answer was characteristic: "Didn't you use to do my printing for me?" asked Dr. Boyd. "Yes, and you always paid your bills." "Haven't I made some real progress in these fifteen years?" "You have grown forty times as fast as I have," was the white printer's reply. "Well," said Dr. Boyd, "I haven't noticed that you waste any time on Bible reading and prayer." I find myself still wondering what the white printer could say in return.

No Final Solution Yet Reached

Of course, one must not conclude from the encouraging facts that have been given above that the question of economic efficiency has been solved for the negro race. One cannot walk the streets of any Southern city and not be impressed with the sight of hundreds of listless, idle and dirty-looking negroes, who not only do not know how to work well, but do not want to learn. I know of nothing that gives one a feeling of more complete helplessness than the seeming dead indifference of thousands of negroes to all the laws of cleanliness, ambition and efficiency. This indifference rests like a great black night on the whole South. As I have said before, the future economic progress of the South is closely knit up with the economic efficiency of the negro, for the negro is now and will, in my judgment, continue to be for the next fifty years, almost our sole dependence for labor. All attempts to import foreign labor into the South have up to the present been almost futile. Even where they have been brought in, the foreigners are unwilling to stay and work in competition with the negro. Our one hope, it seems to me, lies in a more efficient negro laborer. If his indifference and laziness and ignorance cannot be overcome, then we as a section must expect to drop further and further behind in the economic procession of the nation, as the years roll by.

Summary of Principles

Any fair and dispassionate reviewing of the

facts of the present situation, it seems, would justify the following conclusions:

First: We must continue to hold our standards of skill and labor as high as the white laborer can hold them. We dare not think of lowering our standards of efficiency simply because we have among us a large class of less efficient laborers.

Second: We must continue to admit into all forms of employment all who are able to measure up to the standards. This has been our policy in the past and we shall, at our peril, allow any change in this program. If the negro artisan can do the same grade of work as the white man, then public sentiment must continue to demand as it has in the past that he be given a full and free opportunity.

Third: We must give equal wages for equal service. If a negro man can build my house as well as a white man, I must be willing to give him just as good pay. The fact that he has a lower standard of living and can perhaps work for a little less is no excuse for forcing him to continue on this lower plane.

Fourth: We must use every effort to raise the standard of living of the negro artisan to such a place that he cannot afford to work for less money than the white man. This will be to the advantage of the white artisan, for it will obviate unequal and cheap competition; it will be to the advantage of the community at large, for it will give us a larger supply of self-respecting, ambitious and efficient laborers.

Fifth: Equal facilities must be furnished the

members of each race to equip themselves for
the largest possible efficiency. Surely no one can
begrudge any man, whether white or black, a
chance to get that training which will make him
a better workman, a greater producer of wealth,
a more reliable and law-abiding citizen, a greater
force for righteousness, a more self-respecting
man.

Active Advocacy of Principles

For these fundamental principles every Southern white man should stand not only passively
but actively. We should stand for them because
self-preservation can be insured only by such action. We should stand for them because they
are dictated by the laws of a sound economy.
We should stand for them because to do otherwise would be inhuman and far less than Christian.

III

HEALTH AND HOUSING OF THE NEGRO

WE WEAR THE MASK

We wear the mask that grins and lies,
It hides our cheeks and shades our eyes,—
This debt we pay to human guile;
With torn and bleeding hearts we smile,
And mouth with myriad subtleties.

Why should the world be over-wise,
In counting all our tears and sighs?
Nay, let them only see us, while
   We wear the mask.

We smile, but, O great Christ, our cries
To thee from tortured souls arise.
We sing, but oh, the clay is vile
Beneath our feet, and long the mile;
But let the world dream otherwise,
   We wear the mask!

     —PAUL LAURENCE DUNBAR.

HEALTH AND HOUSING OF THE NEGRO

Test of Civilization

The surest test of a civilization lies not in the accumulated wealth of the people, not in the degree of perfection in political organization, not in its educational advancement, and one is tempted to say not even in its organized church life. All of these are, to be sure, indices of development, but the surest test of any civilization lies in the character of its homes. Any race that has the ability to build up and keep sacred the institution of the family must be counted as a progressive race. The past history of the negro has not been very encouraging in this regard. Neither in Africa nor in America during the days of slavery did he know the true meaning of the word home. It is much to the credit of the negro race that out of such a past he is slowly but surely evolving the institutions of the family and the home.

Relation of House to the Home

In this process of evolution, the house in which he lives plays no small part. It has been often and well said that a palace without love and ideals is not a home, and the glory of the one

61

room cottage where love reigns has been sung
by poets and bards. The plain truth, however,
is that one room gives poor opportunity to keep
pure and sweet the love that once entered there,
and the house has more to do with the home than
some poets have dreamed; and surely the house
has a most vital relation to the health and, therefore, to the morals and ideals of its inmates. If
a nation's progress can be measured by its
homes, almost as surely can the state of the
homes be measured by the state of the houses in
which these homes are made. With the idea of
this vital relationship in mind, let us study the
question of negro housing.

Housing in Slavery Days

During the days of slavery, the negroes lived
in the long rows of log cabins—mostly one
roomed—which stretched away from the "big
house" like two white wings. These were known
as the slave quarters, and, being whitewashed,
they not infrequently gave a very picturesque appearance to the old plantation. One who visits
these old Southern plantations to-day may find
the remnants of the slave quarters still in existence, though they are fast tumbling into decay.
In these early days of the South most of the
poorer people of the section lived in these one
or two roomed log cabins; however, the life
therein was cheerless and without comforts.
Booker T. Washington has given a graphic de-
scription of this life in his "Up from Slavery":
"There was a door to the cabin—that is, something that was called a door—but the uncertain

hinges by which it was hung, and the large cracks in it, to say nothing of the fact that it was too small, made the room a very uncomfortable one. In addition to these openings there was, in the lower right-hand corner of the room, the 'cat-hole,'—a contrivance which almost every mansion or cabin in Virginia possessed during the ante-bellum period. The 'cat-hole' was a square opening, about seven by eight inches, provided for the purpose of letting the cat pass in and out of the house at will during the night. In the case of our particular cabin I could never understand the necessity for this convenience, since there were at least a half-dozen other places in the cabin that would have accommodated the cats. There was no wooden floor in our cabin, the naked earth being used as a floor. In the center of the earthen floor there was a large, deep opening covered with boards, which was used as a place in which to store sweet potatoes during the winter. . . ."

This picture drawn by Washington is much more dreary than the average cabin would justify; for usually there was a board floor and somewhat better doors. Life in slave quarters, however, was poor at the best.

Country Housing

The housing conditions of the negro farmer have not changed since slavery nearly so much as one would wish, nor as one might reasonably expect. I have traveled through the country in almost every section of the South, and the negro farm houses consist usually of one, two, or three

rooms, poorly furnished, poorly kept, with no
pictures, and with the barest necessities for living. Professor DuBois has made some study of
a typical slave county — Dougherty County,
Georgia. His word about conditions of housing
is rather pessimistic but is doubtless not much
overdrawn: "The form and disposition of the
laborers' cabins throughout the Black Belt
is to-day the same as in slavery days. Some
live in the self-same cabins, others in cabins re-
built on the sites of the old. All are sprinkled
in little groups over the face of the land, center-
ing about some dilapidated Big House where the
head-tenant or agent lives. The general character and arrangement of these dwellings remains on the whole unaltered. There were in
the country, outside the corporate town of Al-
bany, about fifteen hundred negro families in
1898. Out of all these, only a single family occupied a house with seven rooms; only fourteen
have five rooms or more. The mass live in one-
and two-room houses."

"The size and arrangements of the people's
homes are no unfair index of their condition.
If, then, we inquire more carefully into these
negro homes, we find much that is unsatisfactory. All over the face of the land is the one-
room cabin—now standing in the shadow of the
Big House, now staring at the dusty road, now
rising dark and sombre amid the green of the
cotton-fields. It is nearly always old and bare,
built of rough boards, and neither plastered nor
ceiled. Light and ventilation are supplied by
the single door and by the square hole in the
wall with its wooden shutter. There is no glass,

porch, or ornamentation without. Within is a
fireplace, black and smoky, and usually unsteady
with age. A bed or two, a table, a wooden chest,
and a few chairs compose the furniture; while a
stray show-bill or a newspaper makes up the
decorations for the walls. Now and then one
may find such a cabin kept scrupulously neat,
with merry steaming fireplace and hospitable
door, but the majority are dirty and dilapidated,
smelling of eating and sleeping, poorly ventilated, and anything but homes."

"Above all, the cabins are crowded. We have
come to associate crowding with homes in cities
almost exclusively. This is primarily because
we have so little accurate knowledge of country life. Here in Dougherty county one may
find families of eight and ten occupying one or
two rooms, and for every ten rooms of house ac-
commodation for the negroes there are twenty-
five persons. The worse tenement abominations
of New York do not have above twenty-two
persons for every ten rooms. Of course, one
small, close room in a city, without a yard, is
in many respects worse than the larger single
country room. In other respects it is better;
it has glass windows, a decent chimney, and a
trustworthy floor. The single great advantage
of the negro peasant is that he may spend most
of his life outside his hovel in the open fields."[1]

City Housing

The conditions of houses in themselves are but
lit+le more inviting in the cities. In an investigation of 1,137 negro families made under di-

[1] "Souls of Black Folks," pp. 138-140.

rection of Atlanta University in 1897 it was found that 117 families lived in single-room houses, 276 lived in two-roomed houses, 308 families occupied three rooms each, 197 had four rooms each, 112 had five rooms, 122 had more than five rooms,—and the average number of occupants for all rooms was 2.22 persons. In a study of the Philadelphia negro in 1899 it was found that in the seventh ward alone 829 families, or 35 per cent. of the negro families of the ward, occupied just one room to the family. It is not an uncommon thing for one in passing through the poorer negro section to see a sign, "sleepers wanted," tacked on the front of a two- or three-roomed house occupied by a family of from two to six persons. One house visited had a shed-room, used for a dining-room and kitchen, and two front rooms. In these two front rooms the negro man, his wife, and three grown daughters lived, and they took three "men sleepers" into the house. Another house visited had two rooms—one used for kitchen, dining-room and laundry-room. The wife made the living by taking in washing. In the other room—one without a ray of sunlight—lived this woman, her invalid husband, and two children. In these houses one almost never finds a bath-room and almost as seldom finds a toilet. In the investigation by Atlanta University, of the 1,031 houses visited only 43, or 4 per cent., had bath tubs. It is safe to say that among this class of negroes—the ignorant day-laboring class—this percentage of bath tubs is fully up to the average.

Unfavorable Location

These negro homes have the additional disadvantage of being located in the lower, damper, and more disagreeable parts of the city. In Atlanta, as an illustration, there are large negro settlements in the lower parts of Houston Street, and in the more undesirable parts of West Atlanta. In Nashville, the lowlands between the central part of the city and the residence section of South Nashville, known as "Black Bottom," is tenanted by negroes. So one could go through the list of almost every Southern city, and the facts are always the same.

Still further, these houses are undesirable, because they are largely located on the alleys rather than the streets. Mr. H. Paul Douglass says: "I know a Charleston alley lined with thirty-two negro tenement houses. In the midst of the alley, its sole source of water supply is an open dipping well, surrounded by a sixteen-inch curb. On this curb all the people of the thirty-two houses do their washing, etc."[1] This means that these homes have absolutely no yard space, that they have a most dreary outlook, that they are surrounded by all sorts of unsightly trash, and that the air is not infrequently ladened with foul odors. It would be hard for any people to make homes in such houses. It would be hard to estimate just what would be the deteriorating effect of removing from the homes of our white people every flower, every tree, every blade of grass, and yet that is what has happened for the mass of the negro working-men. Professor DuBois, in his

[1] "Christian Reconstruction in the South," p. 177.

study of the Philadelphia negro, gives the following figures: Of the 1,751 families making returns, 932 had a private yard 12x12 feet, or larger; 312 had a private yard smaller than 12x12 feet; 507 had either no yard or a yard and outhouse in common with the other denizens of the tenement or alley.[1]

Yet again the homes of a large number of negroes are located down in the heart of the city in the old houses long since abandoned by white people, or in those sections of the town where railroads, factories, etc., have made living undesirable.

Lastly, these houses are often old and are kept in poor repair. If it were not for the high rental which they command they would be torn down to give place for better structures.

Exorbitant Rentals

Now the negro not only puts up with these miserable houses and bad locations, but he frequently pays an exorbitant rent. I have asked a good number of landlords why they do not tear away the old negro houses and build decent tenements, and the usual reply is that the present investment brings a larger dividend. Fifteen to twenty per cent. dividends is not thought to be exorbitant from such rentals. In many of the very worst sections of Negrotown in Nashville, rooms rent for two dollars per week. If a woman who is a cook, working for twelve dollars per month, has only one room, she will pay a half to two-thirds of her income for the

---

[1] "The Philadelphia Negro," p. 293.

rent of a miserable hovel. In a recent investigation made in the city of Nashville, out of 12,579 females over fifteen years of age, 5,595 were employed as laundresses, cooks, house girls, and child nurses,—the average salary for which services ranged from eight to fifteen dollars per month. Unless these women had other support than that of their own labor, they would have a bare pittance on which to live after paying room rent. There is no wonder they resort to stealing and even worse crimes.

Why Negroes Accept These Conditions

There are two reasons why negroes will continue to live in these unsanitary houses in the worst sections of the city. In the first place, the great majority of negroes are engaged in personal services, such as that of cooks, waiters, and waitresses, butlers, drivers, nurses, etc. This necessitates their being as near their work as possible. In the second place, the strong social nature of the negro calls for constant companionship. He wants to be where he can see many others of his kind. He does not want to be isolated. Where there are many congregated, there can be some constant amusement. The organ grinder, the medicine man, the street preacher—all of these flourish in the thickly populated sections of the negro district, and to miss these things would be not to live. It is for this reason that people living far out in the suburbs of a city find it difficult to keep negro servants, in spite of the fact that good servants' quarters are furnished. Thousands of negroes

thus live in crowded and unsanitary tenement
houses on the back alleys of the city rather than
live out in the suburbs where they might have
fresh air and sunshine, cheaper rent and a yard
with a garden.

The barest recital of facts such as these con-
vinces one that the negro does not have a chance.
He has had so little and has grown accustomed to
so little that there is danger lest he will not ever
want any better than he has. To increase his
wants, to make him see the blessings of better
houses, and more air and sunshine—this is a
staggering task.

The Better Class of Houses

And, yet, we must not pass without giving
something of the brighter side of the picture.
We are reminded of the 126,329 negro homes
free of debt and owned by negroes. We must
remember that more and more the negro is occupying whole sections of our cities and is making such sections beautiful and attractive. Recently, I went through that section of Atlanta
near Atlanta University where are to be found
the homes of the better class of negroes. The
streets were clean, the yards were green and
well kept, there were plenty of shade trees, and
most of the houses had from four to eight
rooms. They were well painted and one would
hardly have known that it was not a white settlement. Just out by the University, I saw the
handsome new residence of the leading negro
barber of the city,—a brick edifice costing more
than twenty-five thousand dollars. Nor is this
an isolated case. There are such negro settle-

ments in Chattanooga, Nashville, and many other cities that I have visited.

Relation of Health to Housing

In view of what has preceded, one may expect the health of the negro to be below that of the white man. And such is evidently the case. Contrary to the idea of the casual observer, the negro has less of endurance, and his death rate is higher than that of the white man. "The vitality of the negro," says Hoffman,[1] "may well be considered the most important phase of the so-called race problem; for, it is a fact which can, and will, be demonstrated by indisputable evidence, that of all races for which statistics are obtainable, and which enter at all into the consideration of economic problems as factors, the negro shows the least power of resistance in the struggle for life." Mr. Hoffman thinks that this physical weakness of the race presages extermination unless such weakness can be overcome, while others take an opposite view and claim that the birth rate will easily keep in advance of the death rate.

High Death Rate of Negroes

In Washington, for the year 1890, the vital statistics for white and colored showed a relative number of deaths of 67.07 whites to 141.69 colored; and for the same year the figures for Baltimore stood 67.19 whites to 121.55 colored; or, in other words, the negroes in these two

---

[1] "Race Traits and Tendencies of the American Negro," p. 37. I am greatly indebted to this student of the negro for many of the facts in this chapter.

cities that year were twice as unhealthy as the white people. In the cities of Atlanta, Memphis, Charleston, and Richmond, the death rates for the years 1881-1895 were as follows: Atlanta, 18.5 whites to 34.7 colored; Memphis, 20.6 whites to 31.2 colored; Charleston, 23.2 white to 44 colored; Richmond, 20.7 white to 38 colored. Among these cities the comparative death rate most favorable to the negro was in Memphis, where, for every two white deaths per thousand of population, there were three colored deaths; and the least favorable comparative death rate was in Atlanta, where, for every five white deaths per thousand population, there were nine colored deaths. Without wearying the reader with the statistics, it may be stated that both the white death rate and colored death rate in all these cities decreased greatly between 1881 and 1895, but the decrease of the white death rate was greater than that of the colored, hence at the end of the period the latter still stands about 70 per cent. in advance of the former. It may be said also that the statistics of the last census and such other local statistics as are available up to the present year, seem to indicate that this disparity is probably larger now than it was in 1895. Indeed, a number of students of the question have put the death rate per thousand of each race as two to one in favor of the white man.

Causes of Excessive Death Rate

The chief causes of this excessive death rate among negroes seem to be infant mortality, consumption, scrofula, venereal troubles, and intestinal diseases. It will be noted that all of

these are what may be called constitutional diseases, that is, either the disease or else the weakness which makes the subject an easy prey, may
be inherited. Hoffman sums up a number of sta-
tistical tables as giving "evidence that environment has less effect on the duration of life than
have the factors of race and heredity."[1]

Infant Mortality

The infant mortality among the peoples in
America is alarmingly high. Too little attention has been paid in the past to the feeding
and care of infants. Among the colored people
this mortality is still further marked. As illus-
trations of this fact, the following statistics for
the year 1890 may be cited: New Orleans, 1,290
colored births, 555 of which children died before
one year of age, or a death rate of 430.2 per thousand; Charleston, 758 births, 350 of whom died
under one year of age, or a rate of 461.7; Richmond, 625 births, 331 deaths, death rate of infants, 529.6 per thousand. In other words, of
every two colored children born only one lives to
be one year old. This is a death plague almost
like that visited upon the children of Egypt by
the destroying angel.

Neglect of Children

For this alarming infant mortality there are
three chief causes: First, the mother works out
and must leave the infant in the care of other
children who are too young to give it proper attention. According to statistics quoted before,
44 per cent. of the negro women in Nashville

---

[1] "Race Traits and Tendencies," p. 51.

over fifteen years of age are employed as laundresses, cooks, housemaids, and child nurses,
which means that in most cases they must leave
their own children without proper care during
the day. It may also be added that the medical
care given to negro children is altogether in-
adequate. Thousands of them die without ever
being seen by a physician. Here is a crying need
for more trained negro physicians who can, and
will, meet this need of humanity. These facts
will undoubtedly account for much of this excessive infant mortality. As to the other great
causes of high death rate among infants, let a
negro speak, lest we shall be charged with unfair
judgment.[1]

Immorality and Child Diseases

"There is one obstacle in the race's reproduc-
ing itself that has some connection with venereal
diseases and hence I speak of it now. I refer to the
enormous amount of still births and infant mortality prevalent everywhere among colored people. For the period of 1893-95, the still and premature births in the city of Nashville were 272 for
the white, and 385 for the colored; or, in proportion to the population, two and one-third times as
many as there ought to have been. This relative
state of affairs obtains in Memphis and Atlanta,
and in all the large cities of the South. From the
health reports of all our large Southern cities we
learn that a considerable amount of our infant
mortality is due to inanition, infantile debility,
and infantile marasmus. Now, what is the case

---

[1] "Social and Physical Conditions of Negroes in
Cities," p. 24.

in regard to these diseases? The fact is that
they are not diseases at all, but merely the names
of symptoms due to enfeebled constitutions and
congenital diseases inherited from parents suffering from the effects of sexual immorality and
debauchery. Translated into common speech,
they are nothing more than infant starvation, infant weakness, and infant wasting away, the
cause of which is that the infants' parents before them have not given them a fighting chance
for life. According to Hoffman, over 50 per
cent. of the negro children born in Richmond,
Va., die before they are one year old.

"The number of still and premature births
among us is a matter of great alarm, not only because it seriously interferes with the numerical
increase of the race, but because it involves the
fecundity, the health, and even the moral character of large numbers of our women. The support of the family often falls very heavily upon
our poor washerwomen; and since they find it
hard to get the husks to feed and the rags to
clothe their already large number of little folks,
living in one room like stock, rather than add
to their burden, they resort to crime. An official
on the Nashville Board of Health, who is also
proprietor of a drug store, tells me that he is
astonished at the number of colored women who
apply at his store for drugs with a criminal purpose in view."

Prevalence of Consumption

A second cause of excessive death rate among
negroes is consumption. According to the census
of 1890, the mortality from consumption per

100,000 of each race in certain typical cities was as follows:[1]

	White.	Colored.
Charleston, S. C.	355.4	686.3
New Orleans, La.	250.3	587.7
Savannah, Ga	371.1	54.4
Mobile, Ala.	304.1	608.2
Atlanta, Ga.	213.8	483.7
Richmond, Va.	230.5	411.1
Washington, D. C.	245	591.8

It will be seen from this table that the lowest excess for the colored deaths over white from consumption is 74 per cent. in Richmond, and the highest excess is 136 per cent. in the City of New Orleans. Not only is this death rate very much higher, but it seems to be increasing. The figures from the City of Charleston, from 1822 or 1894, will indicate this:[2]

CONSUMPTION IN CHARLESTON, S. C., 1822-1894

(Death rates per 100,000 of population).

Period.	White.	Colored.
1822-30	457	447
1831-40	331	320
1841-48	268	266
1865-74	198	411
1875-84	255	668
1885-94	189	627

[1] Figures taken from "Race Traits and Tendencies of American Negro," p. 83.

[2] Figures copied from "Race Traits and Tendencies of American Negro," p. 70.

Thus, while the consumptive death rate, 1822-30, was about equal for whites and blacks, that of the blacks was nearly three and one-third times as great as that of the whites for the period 1885-1894. It seems quite evident that consumption is very much more prevalent since slavery than during slave days.

Predisposition to Consumption

Hoffman thinks the negro has a predisposition to consumption, the conclusions concerning which he sums up the following words:[1] "The average girth of chest of the negro male of thirty years ago was slightly greater than that of the white, but at the present time the chest expansion of the colored male is less than that of the white. This decrease in the size of the living thorax in part explains the increase in the mortality from consumption and respiratory diseases."

"The capacity of the lungs of the negro is considerably below that of the white. This fact, coupled with the smaller weight of the lungs (4 oz.), is without question another powerful factor in the great mortality from diseases of the lungs." There can be little doubt that one cause of depleted lung power and hence of increased consumption, may be the foul atmosphere in the midst of which so many negroes live.

These facts will only explain the prevalence of the disease and not its increase. The reason for the increase of the disease among negroes may possibly be found in the increase of that other group of diseases, scrofula, syphilis and gon-

---

[1] "Race Traits and Tendencies," p. 170.

orrhea. These diseases are known to be veritable scourges among the colored population. I have taken pains to question a great many Christian physicians, both white and colored, about the prevalence of gonorrhea among negroes, and most of them put the percentage among the men at ninety-five out of every hundred. Some of the colored physicians have put it higher than that. There can, of course, be no reliable statistics secured on this point, and these are simply opinions which cannot be verified. It is always dangerous to accept opinions as verified facts: but, allowing for all error, the figures must be alarmingly high. Let us turn to the Atlanta University investigation, which was made by negroes, to find their opinion about the increase and deadliness of these diseases among their own race:[1] "For the period 1882-85, the colored death rate in Memphis from scrofula and syphilis was 205.8 per cent. in excess of that among the whites; but from 1891 down to the present time, the excess has been 298 per cent. For the period 1893-95, there were in the City of Nashville 8 white deaths from scrofula and syphilis, and 35 colored. In proportion to the population there ought to have been only 5 colored. Of course, allowance must be made for the fact that, on account of the scandal and disgrace, white physicians are reluctant to report white deaths from these causes; whereas such motives rarely, if ever, influence them in reporting colored deaths."

[1] "Social and Physical Condition of Negroes in Cities," p. 23.

Scrofula and Syphilis

"According to the May Bulletin of the Department of Labor, out of 1,090 colored people canvassed this year in the City of Nashville, 18 were suffering from scrofula and syphilis. One whose attention has not been called to the matter has no conception of the prevalence of these diseases among the negroes of Nashville. I have looked for it in both races as I have walked the streets of my city, and to come across the loathsome disease in the colored passers-by is not an uncommon occurrence. This state of affairs can be accounted for when I tell you that there is probably no city in this country where prostitution among colored people is more rampant and brazen, and where abandoned colored women are more numerous or more public in their shameful traffic."

Inferences

It would seem to be a fair conclusion from these facts that sexual immorality among negroes is so debilitating the mothers and fathers, that a large percentage of the children are born dead, or else they enter the world so starved and diseased that half of them die before they reach the age of one year.

Further, it may be concluded that this sexual immorality is so sapping the vital power of the negro race that they fall an easy prey to diseases such as consumption, and when once such a disease has got hold of their lives they have not the vital power to withstand or check its ravages. And, lastly, one may conclude that the diseases which arise out of sexual immorality are taking off large numbers of the race to premature graves. Here is a sight loathsome enough to sicken even the stoutest heart. A race of people in our very midst, many of them working in our own homes, and yet dying of a more awful leprosy than one dare describe—a leprosy all the more deadly because it kills not only the body but damns the soul.

Housing and Health

What relationship has the housing question to these questions of health and morals? A very vital one, and yet, perhaps, not just the relation which has been so commonly in mind. It is not fevers alone that arise out of housing conditions, though such conditions may be directly responsible for a large portion of such diseases. Poor housing, back alleys, no ventilation, poor sanitation, no sunshine do much to foster disease of all kinds. In particular they prepare fertile soil for the growth of the tubercular germs. They weaken the body of the inhabitant so that he is not best able to withstand disease. They may so discourage the people who dwell in such surroundings that they do not struggle against the ravages of sickness.

Housing and Morals

But these are not the worst results of the overcrowding and poor housing. By far the worst results on health arise out of the low state of morals they superinduce. So long as people are huddled together in filthy houses and unsanitary surroundings, so long will they be lacking in that pride and self-respect which makes for morality.

A man living on a clean street—all other things being equal—is a more decent and moral man than he would be were he living on a back alley. A man who has had a bath is surely more apt to have clean thoughts than the man who never bathes. The man who wears decent clothes in keeping with his decent surroundings has a better chance to be moral than the man who is filthy in the midst of filthy surroundings. No man who has ever shaved and bathed and donned clean linen can for one moment fail to understand that cleanliness not only is next to godliness, but cleanliness helps to create godliness. We cannot make people moral so long as they live in filth and in squalid surroundings.

Further, people cannot be moral so long as they are herded together like cattle without privacy or decency. If the men and the women, the boys and the girls from half a dozen tenements are forced to use one toilet, we cannot expect either privacy or decency. If a mother, a father, three grown daughters, and men boarders have to sleep in two small rooms, we must expect lack of modesty, promiscuity, illegitimacy and sexual diseases. It would be a miracle if it turned out otherwise. No nation in modern times can live and be moral when its people eat and drink, work and sleep, bring forth children and come to death in one-room cabins. A one-room house, however clean, is not conducive to family morality, and the sooner we realize this and have some measure of sympathy for the weakness of people who live under such conditions, the sooner will we take steps to make conditions of life for the negro such as will be more conducive to morality.

After all, the question of negro health and housing is a moral question. His present mode of life is such as to render it well nigh impossible for him to be moral, and his present immorality makes him an inefficient laborer, an expensive criminal, a distributor of infectious diseases, and a moral plague. We are—whether we like it or not—bound in the matter of self-defense, to see that these conditions are changed. He must have a new sense of personal purity, he must have a new sense of the sacredness of the family relations, he must come to have a new pride in his home. To this end the houses in which he lives must be improved, the streets on which his house stands must be cleaner, and the sanitation in his section of the city must be made equal to that of any other section of the city in which he lives.

Common Sense Policy

It is not maudlin sentiment that dictates such a policy; it is sane commonsense. It is the law of economics which demands strong, healthy and efficient labor; it is the law of self-preservation which knows the danger of social contamination; it is the law of justice which would give to every man, whether rich or poor, learned or ignorant, white or black, an equal chance to achieve, and that under the fairest conditions; it is these laws and not sentiment that demand the betterment of the negro's condition.

Hopeful Signs

Through the darkness of the present condition there are two rays of light. The first is the

awakening conscience of a respectable minority
of the colored race, who are making a heroic
fight to preserve their own purity of life, and doing what they can to lift their race out of the
mire. All honor to the little band of brave,
heroic souls. It is a battle worthy of the best
steel. Here and there I have met these moral
heroes, and their bold, hopeful courage in the
presence of such difficulties is a tonic to the faith
of any man. He who would scorn such a fighter
or laugh at his failures and mistakes has not
the spirit of true chivalry in his heart. Would
that we had more men who labored as unselfishly
for what they conceive to be the good of their
people, as are Washington, DuBois, Gilbert,
Hunton, Hope and scores of others less promin-
ent, but no less earnest.

The second ray of light emanates from the
awakening responsibility of the white man. As
I have traveled from college to college, here and
there I have found college men that really cared,
men that saw the dire need of these "neighbors
in black," and began to stretch out a hand to
them. It is not strange—it is what one would
expect—that this generation of college men are
more interested in these human beings by their
sides than any other class of men, and the time
will come when every college man will see that
his larger culture, his better chance, his broader
outlook—all these put him under obligation to
help the race that is down.

IV

THE EDUCATION OF THE NEGRO

UNEXPRESSED

Deep in my heart that aches with the repression,
  And strives with plenitude of bitter pain,
There lives a thought that clamors for expression,
  And spends its undelivered force in vain.

What boots it that some other may have thought it?
  The right of thoughts' expression is divine;
The price of pain I pay for it has bought it,
  I care not who lays claim to it—'tis mine!

And yet not mine until it be delivered;
  The manner of its birth shall prove the test.
Alas, alas, my rock of pride is shivered—
  I beat my brow—the thought still unexpressed.

              —PAUL LAURENCE DUNBAR.

IV

THE EDUCATION OF THE NEGRO

Prejudice Against Education

Aside from the question of social inter-mingling, perhaps the question of negro education has aroused more prejudice and created more discussion than any other in connection with the race problem. Those who have studied the prevailing opinion among Southern whites must recognize that there is little enthusiasm for the educated negro. As a civilized nation we have long since accepted the maxim that "knowledge is power," and that any nation which keeps its people in ignorance is doomed to mediocrity. But somehow we have not applied this thought to the colored race of America. Perhaps this attitude has arisen out of the fear that education will lead to negro dominance in politics and to promiscuous mingling in social life. The Southern white man will never be enthusiastic for negro education until he is convinced that such education will not lead to either of these. Neither will he become enthusiastic until he finds the trained negro becoming a more efficient workman and a better citizen. The *so-called* educated negro has not always proven himself a better laborer or a better citizen. This, perhaps, is

the fault neither of education nor of the negro—
it is the fault of mistaken ideas of what constitutes education. There has been much said
about the decrease of illiteracy among negroes
from somewhere between 90 per cent. and 100
per cent in 1865, to only 43 per cent. in 1909.
This is a marvelous development, and is a long
step toward education. To be able to read and
write opens up an entirely new world to men. It
is as though one opened the eyes of the blind or
unstopped the ears of the deaf. But I can easily
understand that the discordant noises of the
world would break with great harshness on those
ears which had always been closed, and the soul
with this new gateway of knowledge suddenly
opened would be completely bewildered and fail
to understand the meaning of all these conflict-
ing noises. So it is with the negro who has just
come into possession of the use of these strange
symbols that we call an alphabet. He is not
at once transformed into a man with a cultured
mind; he must be bewildered by much that he
reads, having no key to its real understanding.
Education for the negro has not been tried, for
the little smattering of knowledge which he has
may well have bewildered him rather than cleared
his thought.

Present Negroes vs. Slave Negroes

It is not unlikely that the negro is more immoral to-day than he was during slavery days—
now that he is all too free. Neither can it be
denied that the mass of negroes were better
trained workmen during slavery days than now,

even though in slavery days nine out of every ten were illiterate. Not infrequently men have jumped to the conclusion that the cause of the immorality and of the economic inefficiency is education. This, however, is an entirely unwarranted conclusion.

Unfounded Argument

"These opponents of negro education, with the lack of logic characteristic of the man who draws general conclusions from a few particulars and sees only what is superficially discernible without looking for deeper and more far-reaching causes, ascribe the cause of this difference to the little education that the negro has received. The modern negro has had some sort of education and the old-issue negro had none, therefore they argue education is the cause of the inferiority of the modern negro. They forget that the best of the old negroes were trained in the best industrial schools, on farms and in shops, for the work they were to do in life, under the direction of intelligent masters; that in many instances the intimacy of relations between them and the families of humane masters afforded them an environment, association and example that proved most potent in shaping and strengthening their characters; and that the whole social system of the old *régime* was conducive to training the negroes in obedience, self-restraint and industry. Though these old negroes were ignorant of books, they were, from earliest infancy, trained and educated in many of the essentials of good citizenship and efficient service. The present generation of negroes have been given a mere smattering of the unessentials of knowledge, and left untrained in those other things so essential to life and happiness and progress. The new generation, without preparation, were ushered into freedom and have been left to follow largely their own will without direction or restraint, save that of the criminal law, without elevating associations, without leaders or teachers, save a few rare exceptions."

Need of Practical Demonstration

"We cannot answer effectively this prejudice against negro education, arising from the results produced by causes largely attributable, perhaps, to revolutionized social, political and industrial conditions wrought by the tornado of civil war, save with a practical demonstration of the better results of a better education. All the evils of a reconstruction of society, life and government upon a weak race unprepared for such changes, ushered into the new order of things with but few intelligent, wise, right-thinking leaders, without power of proper self-restraint or self-direction, have been laid by the demagogues, by the unthinking, and by some other men and women as honest and patriotic as any that breathe, at the door of partial education as the quickest, easiest and most plausible solution of the unsatisfactory results. Too few stop to think what might have been the result if the new generation of negroes had been allowed to grow up in absolute ignorance under these changed conditions, with the rights and freedom of citizens of a republic, without the restraint of the training and the association of educated masters, as under the old system. Too few stop to think that whatever of deterioration there may have been in the new generation of negroes, as compared with the old, may be more attributable to a change in civilization and in the whole order of things than to the little learning that he has received. Too few stop to think of the danger and the unfairness of the sort of reasoning that compares the best of the old generation of negroes with the worst of the new, that compares the partly educated negro of the present generation with the illiterate negro of the old generation, who, though ignorant of books, had much knowledge of many useful industries and trades and better opportunities of acquiring such knowledge; instead of comparing the literate negro of the new generation with the illiterate negro of the new generation, that ascribes all the faults found in the new generation to the smattering of learning that they have received and all the virtues found in the old generation to their illiteracy. One is partly educated, the other was illiterate; therefore education is the cause of the faults of the one and illiteracy of the virtues of the other. The absurdity of such logic ought to be manifest to the average man. Here are two men, one educated, the other ignorant. One becomes a murderer, for there have been educated murderers in all times; the other becomes a good citizen, for there have been ignorant good citizens in all times; therefore education makes murderers and ignorance makes good citizens."[1]

---

[1] Report of North Carolina Superintendent of Public Instruction. 1906-7; 1907-8, pp. 44, 45.

Reconstruction and Prejudice Against Education

Another cause for prejudice against negro education arises out of its checkered career during reconstruction days. At that particular time the relationship between the Northern white and the Southern white man was greatly strained. The North suspected the South of keeping the negro in ignorance in order that he might be exploited; and the South suspected the North of trying to educate the negro in order that he might have political dominion and sooner or later lay claim to so-called social equality. Both sides were in a measure right and it is certain now that both were in a measure wrong. It is usually an unsafe thing to condemn wholesale the motives and the judgment of the people of a whole section, whether North or South. Nevertheless, in the passion of the times, many mistakes were made by the missionaries who came South, which completely alienated the Southern whites, and it is only within the last decade that this gulf has been at all adaquately bridged. Even now there are not a few sincere Southern men who confuse negro education with doctrines of social intermingling. It is now time we were forgetting this feeling and facing like men the question of negro education on its merits, without reference to the mistakes of the past, save in so far as they may serve as warnings for the present.

Education in Slave Days

The history of negro education before the Civil War is very checkered and also very meager. It was not thought wise to educate the slaves lest they might become restive, hence one State after another, both North and South, put laws on their statute books forbidding the teaching of negroes. In 1740 South Carolina passed a law with the following provisions:

"Whereas, the having of slaves taught to write, or suffering them to be employed in writing, may be attended with inconvenience be it enacted, That all and any person or persons whatsoever, who shall hereafter teach, or cause any slave or slaves to be taught, or shall use or employ any slave as scribe in any manner of writing whatever, hereafter taught to write, every such person or persons shall for every such offense forfeit the sum of 100 pounds current money." [1]

In 1831 Virginia followed suit with the following law:

"That all meetings of free negroes or mulattoes at any school house, church, meeting-house or other place for teaching them reading or writing, either in the day or night, under whatsoever pretext, shall be deemed an unlawful assembly. . . . If any white person or persons assemble with free negroes or mulattoes at any school house, church, meeting-house, or other place for the purpose of instructing such free negroes or mulattoes to read or write, such person or persons shall, on conviction thereof, be fined a sum not exceeding $50, and, moreover, may be imprisoned, at the discretion of a jury, not exceeding two months." [2]

---

[1] "Race Adjustment."—Miller. p. 251.
[2] Ibid. p. 252.

In 1829 Georgia put on her statute books a law which reads as follows:

"If any slave, negro, or free person of color, or any white person, shall teach any other slave, negro, or free person of color to read or write, either written or printed characters, the said free person of color or slave shall be punished by fine and whipping, or fine or whipping, at the discretion of the court; and if a white person so offend he, she, or they shall be punished with a fine not exceeding $500 and imprisonment in the common jail, at the discretion of the court."[1]

Mississippi, North Carolina, Kentucky and Louisiana in establishing their systems of public education between 1830 and 1840 all discriminated against the colored race.

In spite of these facts, however, there were a number of schools in existence before 1860 for the training of the children of freedmen. It is estimated that in the slave States at the opening of the war there were no less than 4,000 free colored children in school.

Freedman's Bureau

The second period of negro education extends from 1860 to 1875. This is the period of the army schools, the Freedman's Bureau, and of Northern domination. The "army schools," as they were called, were made up of those negroes who fled to the Federal armies and were organizd into schools. When the Freedman's Bureau opened work in 1866, these schools had in attendance nearly one hundred thousand. When Gen-

---

[1] "Race Adjustment."—Miller, p. 248.

eral O. O. Howard was put in charge of the Freedman's Bureau he took over these schools, gave them a better organization, doubled their attendance, and brought in a large number of the best young women of the North as teachers. That these schools did not do all that could be expected was surely not due to the lack of unselfishness on the part of these teachers.

Period of Industrialism

About 1870 the Southern States began establishing schools for negroes, and by 1875 a constructive policy was in the making. With the establishment of Hampton Institute a new type of education came into vogue, which has greatly influenced all subsequent educational methods. The third period of negro education, therefore, has been marked by a decided tendency toward industrialism. This tendency has been constantly accentuated as the industrial awakening of the South has been more and more pronounced.

A Dual System of Schools

It was during this period that the South came to realize the stupendous task that lay before her in educating two races in separate school systems, and yet with heroism the men of this section have set their faces forward and they will not turn back. This dual system has been expensive in a country so sparsely settled as the South, and it is but natural that it should have meant poorer schools, shorter terms and more meager salaries. Nevertheless it has been a necessity. In many of the counties of the South there are two, three or

even ten negroes to every white man, and to mix
the schools in these sections would be to reduce
the more advanced race to the station of the less
advanced.

This would be an expensive process both for
the white and the colored race. If the colored
race is to find its largest progress, it must be
through the inspiration and help of the more
cultured race, and that race to give its best, needs
to have opportunity to develop its children under
the most favorable conditions. Not only so, but
the negro has gained in that he has had a chance
to furnish the teachers and leaders for his own
race. This has set a goal of ambition for the
negro youth, and has meant much to engender a
real race pride. Had the races been educated together, the schools would have had white
teachers, and the negro would have lost this advantage. Under the heavy burden of a double
school system the South has moved steadily and
bravely forward.

Elementary Education Needed

Three types of education are needed for the
negro of the South. The first is that of the
elementary public school. This the South has
deliberately set out to furnish. According to the
Report of the United States Commissioner of
Education for 1909, there were in the former
slave States 3,054,888 negro children between
the ages of five and eighteen. Of this number
1,659,217, or about 54 per cent., were enrolled in
the common schools of these States. Including
the numbers in two or three of the border States,

there were 3,114 male teachers and 5,886 female teachers in charge of these children. All of the Southern States do not keep separate records of expenditures for the education of the two races, so no exact amount can be given. North Carolina does keep such a record. This State had 231,801 colored children of school age in 1908, as compared with 483,915 white children. For the colored children the State spent on common schools $366,734.28, as compared with $1,851,- 376.57 for white children. In other words, for less than half the number of children about one-fifth of the amount spent for whites was spent on colored schools. The expenditure per colored child was $1.58, that for each white child of school age, $3.82. If this same proportion holds for the other former slave States, the total expenditure for negro common schools for 1907-8 would be $12,487.079. Of course, one cannot be sure that this is even an approximately close estimate. The total amount of money spent in the common schools of these former slave States since 1870 is $979,831,485. If one-fifth of this has been spent on negro schools—which is probably too large an estimate—the amount would be $195,966,097. This would be really an enormous sum spent by the white people of the South on the education of the negro, particularly when we consider the poverty which has prevailed in this section up to within the last few years.

The Negro's Share

Of this amount the negro is beginning to pay a fair proportion. Thus, in 1908, in North Car-

olina, the negroes paid in taxes $147,949 toward
the $366,734.28 spent on their schools. In this
connection it must be noted that $1.58 is a very
paltry sum to spend on the education of a child
each year. At this rate between the ages of five
and eighteen, the State would spend on every
child $20.12. But New York and Massachusetts
each spend $27 yearly on every child of school
age, and the District of Columbia spends $35.21,
and yet North Carolina's school tax is heavier
than that of Massachusetts. While the South,
therefore, is making a heroic effort to give the
common school to the negro, the results are
nothing less than pitiable. As the wealth of the
section grows, there must be heavier school taxes
if we are to do our duty by these backward
people.

Limitations

The outcome of these meager appropriations
can readily be seen in the length of term and
salary of teachers. The average length of term
for rural colored schools in North Carolina in
1908 was 82.1 days, and the average length for
all colored schools, including city high schools,
was only 93 days. The average monthly salary of
rural colored teachers this same year was $22.48,
and for city colored teachers it was $30.20.
There are still 195 log school houses for colored
children in the State, and 2,216 of the negro
school houses are still furnished with home-
made desks and benches. I have before me the
reports from almost every Southern State and
the figures are often much lower. Thus, in

Georgia, the average length of term for white children is 59 days, and for colored children 40 days. The salaries paid, however, are somewhat higher, being $37.65 per month for negro men, and $27.22 per month for negro women. In most of the States only about 50 per cent. of the negro children attend school, and then the school houses are overcrowded. In some of our Southern cities I am told there are three children for every seat in a colored school house if they all should really attend. These statements are surely enough to show a great need for better educational equipment. Of the need for better teachers we will speak later.

Contribution of Public Schools

The contribution which the negro common school makes to the civilizing and elevating of the negro, Mr. Edgar Gardner Murphy puts in the four following statements:

1. "It represents the discipline of punctuality. When the untutored child first gets into his mind the notion of going to a particular place and of doing a particular thing at a particular time, he has begun to get into line with conscious, intelligent, efficient human life. In other words, he has got hold of one of the rudimentary assumptions of civilization."

2. "It stands also for the discipline of order. The child finds not only that there is a time to come and a time to go, but that there is a place to sit and a place not to sit. He finds that there is a place for everything, that everything has its place, and that even standing and sitting, as well

as the whole task of behaving, are to be performed under the control and direction of another.

3. "The primary school stands also for the discipline of silence. For a group of chattering children—negro children, any children—there is a moral value in the discipline of silence. To learn how to keep still, to learn the lesson of self-containment and self-command, to get hold of the power of that personal calm which is half modesty and half courage, to learn a little of the meaning of quiet and something of the secret of listening—this is an element in that supremacy of will which is the faculty and privilege of the civilized.

4. "Finally, the primary school stands for the discipline of association. It represents the idea of getting together. Getting together is a civilizing exercise. Ten people, old or young, cannot get together in a common room for a common purpose without every one's yielding something for the sake of others—some whim, some impulse of restlessness, some specific convenience, or some personal comfort. Human society is a moral achievement. Associated effort, however slight the sphere of its exercise, represents part of the discipline of civilization." [1]

Industrial Schools Needed

The second type of school needed for the negro is that which gives industrial training. In fact every common school should have some industrial features. One of the charges brought against

[1] "The Present South."—Murphy. p. 73.

the public schools, both for whites and blacks, is that they train children away from the practical interests of life. This practical side may easily be exaggerated, and our schools drift into simple bread and butter machines, without any of the cultural value which should pertain to any education; nevertheless, there is need that we shall guard against a too theoretical system of education.

There is peculiar need to guard this point with the negro child since his new freedom has begotten a disposition to despise all labor. He must be taught that labor is sacred and that honest toil never degrades. If he is to have this attitude toward labor, he must be taught to use skill in his work, to take pride in his ability to do it better than others could do it. Possibly no section of the country is so greatly in need of skilled industrial laborers to-day as is the South. The marvelous growth of the cotton mills during the last two decades is the wonder of the manufacturing world. The new demands for intensive farming make it imperative that we shall have better trained agriculturists. The development of building industries calls for thousands of skilled carpenters, masons, bricklayers, plumbers, painters, etc. Much of this work must be done by colored men. If they are not well trained, our farms will produce one-half or one-third of what they ought to produce, our houses will be poorly built, and every industrial interest of our country will languish. Booker T. Washington has characterized industrial education as having these functions: (1) "To teach the dignity of labor";

(2) "To teach the trades thoroughly and effectively"; (3) "To supply the demand for trained industrial leaders."[1]

South an Agricultural Section

The South is still largely an agricultural section. This is peculiarly true of the colored South. In spite of the rapid drift of the negro to the city, probably 80 per cent. of the colored laborers are on the farms. This means they must have some special training in agriculture. They must learn how to make two blades of grass grow where formerly only one grew. If this is to come about, every negro leader must have a deeper sympathy for this industrial life. Booker T. Washington puts it thus strongly:

"I do not want to startle you when I say it, but I should like to see during the next fifty years every colored minister and teacher, whose work lies outside the large cities, armed with a thorough knowledge of theoretical and practical agriculture, in connection with his theological and academic training. This, I believe, should be so because the race is an agricultural one, and because my hope is that it will remain such. Upon this foundation almost every race in history has got its start. With cheap lands, a beautiful climate and a rich soil, we can lay the foundation of a great and powerful race. The question that confronts us is whether we will take advantage of this opportunity?"[2]

[1] "Working with Hands," p. 80.
[2] "Character Building," p. 262.

Public Schools Not Industrial Schools

Now the negro common or public school has not been able, up to the present time, to meet this need, because of small means. Superintendent Joyner puts it thus: "When we are appropriating only $366,734.28 for the education of 231,801 negro children, we need not be entertaining many hopes of giving the negro much helpful industrial training yet, for everybody ought to know that this amount is not sufficient to give this number of children thorough instruction in the mere rudiments of reading, writing and arithmetic, so essential to civilized living and intelligent service in the humblest callings of life."[1]

Jeanes Foundation

In order to meet this pressing need for agricultural and industrial training, Miss Anna T. Jeanes has set aside a fund of $1,000,000, the interest on which is to be applied in aiding rural schools. Prof. James H. Dillard, formerly Dean of the Academic Department of Tulane University, is the president and general agent for the Jeanes Foundation. The methods of work of this Foundation can be gathered from Professor Dillard's report on the work done in Henrico County, Va., during the year 1908-9:

"We supplied the county superintendent with the salary for a competent teacher, whose duty it should be to introduce industrial work into the twenty-two colored rural schools of the county, and to supervise the work. This teacher, Miss

---

[1] "Report of Superintendent of Public Schools of North Carolina." 1907-8, p. 43.

Virginia E. Randolph, began work on October 26, 1908, and the schools closed June 1. She has spent her whole time in visiting these schools, sometimes two or three a day, so that the schools have had the benefit, not only of the industrial training, but of constant supervision, suggestion and encouragement. It has also been a part of her work to form in the various communities, organizations for school and home improvement.

Miss Randolph writes me that the work of the schools is now on exhibition at the Henrico County Court House, and that the members of the Henrico board are agreeably surprised. I can state from letters received that the work is very heartily approved by the county superintendent.

"There are very many counties in which it would be impossible at present to carry out this plan. Whether from lack of schools, or the wide separation of those that exist, or the shortness of term, or the incompetence of the teachers, the plan would not yet be feasible. I find, however, that it will be possible in many places to adopt a modification of the plan; that is, we can supply the salary for a teacher at the most favorable point in the county, have this teacher give three or four days' work to this school, and let her give the rest of her time to two, three or four neighboring schools, with the intention of influencing these schools and communities in the same manner as has been done in Henrico County." [1]

[1] "Report of United States Commissioner of Education." 1909. Vol. I, pp. 235-6.

Other Form of Help

During the first year of the work of this Foundation, ending July, 1909, $15,059 was thus spent in teachers' salaries, supplementing the common school with special industrial instruction. It is much to be regretted that the fund is not much larger in order that this work might be greatly multiplied.

Training Leaders

To supply the leaders in this industrial education the country has to look to such schools as Hampton Institute in Virginia, and Tuskegee in Alabama. We are scarcely aware of the debt of gratitude we owe to these two schools and to those newer ones that are trying to embody their ideals. The ideal of these schools is to make men efficient, to teach them the dignity of labor, to inculcate the ideal of service, and to make real to every student his duties to God and man. Some people have found fault with Tuskegee because it has not trained servants for our homes. It has done a much more important thing. It has sent out hundreds of graduates who have become the foremost leaders of their race—training them to be industrious, to work regularly and to work efficiently. It is a better thing for a girl that graduates from Tuskegee to spend her energies teaching other women how to cook and sew well than to spend her time in one white man's kitchen. Ultimately we reap the benefit in the form of a better trained laboring class. Booker T. Washington has so admirably described the purposes of this type of school in his introductory chapter to "Working with Hands," that I could wish that every Southern man would read it carefully.

Special Training Needed

The third type of negro education needed is what we may call collegiate training. Against this type of education there has been much opposition and prejudice. I suppose there is no doubt that it has at times been over emphasized and that students poorly qualified have been allowed to enter such courses. The negro, however has no monopoly of this false policy in the South, where there are white colleges that take men from the plow handles and teach them everything from their letters "plumb through" to the final touches of classic lore in the remarkably short time of four years. That there have been mistakes made in negro education cannot be doubted. The question for us to consider, however, is what are the needs of a rightly directed collegiate training for negroes. It seems to me there are three classes of men that must have advanced training; these are the ministers, the teachers and the professional class, including physicians and dentists.

Policy of Self Help

It is a well established policy of all missionary work to put the burden of responsibility on the natives just as rapidly as representative leaders can be trained for these tasks. The same policy has been followed in the South with regard to the negro. We have turned over to the negro preacher the development of the religious and moral life of his race; to the teacher the development of its intellectual life; and as rapidly as possible we are turning over to their physicians and dentists the care of the physical well-being of the negro. This is just as it should be, but the questions of supreme importance both to the colored man and to the white man are: Are these leaders competent to do their work? Are they sufficiently educated to have broad sympathies and clear judgment? Can they be trusted in times of crises to lead their people aright? These are questions of tremendous import. In the answer to them much of the well-being and peace of the South depends.

Trained Ministers Needed

As we shall see in a later chapter the negro minister is all too frequently ignorant, prejudiced, emotional, and even immoral. Education does not always change a man's morals, and yet it may be said to the credit of the negro educated ministers, that they stand head and shoulders above the general mass in morals and in fair mindedness. No negro minister can be a good leader of his people who does not know the moving of God in history. He must have thorough training in the Bible. He must have some acquaintance with the laws of human life. In short, the negro minister must have much of the same kind of training that our white ministers need, with the exception, perhaps, of the languages. Be it said to the credit of most of the negro colleges they jut more stress on English, history and

economics than on the more impractical branches.
I confess I am disappointed that some of the
catalogues seem to indicate an overfondness for
Latin and Greek. This, however, will be righted
when the Southern white man gives sufficient
study to this whole question to be able to give
sane counsel.

Physicians and Dentists Needed

In another chapter we have referred to the need
of better medical attention among negroes. This
can be had only through a well trained medical
and dental fraternity of the negro race. For this
purpose we must have well equipped and well
endowed medical and dental colleges.

Trained Teachers Needed

Lastly, we must have better trained negro
teachers. According to the State School Commissioner of Georgia, the number of negro
teachers in that State holding normal certificates
in 1908 was only 326. Only 129 held first grade
certificates, 476 held second grade certificates,
while the vast majority, 2,037, held third grade
certificates. When one remembers the exceedingly low requirements for a third grade certif-
icate, it is no wonder that negro education is so
inefficient, and apparently shows such poor
results.

Broad Culture Needed

It is coming to be a maxim of good education
that the elementary teacher needs as broad culture and as thorough training as the teacher in

higher branches. Otherwise the teaching in the lower grades becomes simply a process of questions and answers, according to the letter of the text book. In order that there may be a more thorough uplift of the negro child there must be a better training of the negro teacher.

Schools of Advanced Standing

Now of all the schools that are attempting to do work of high school grade and upward, not counting public schools, including all the industrial schools, such as Tuskegee, there are in the former slave States, plus those in Ohio, Pennsylvania, Delaware, New Jersey and Oklahoma, just 135 institutions, according to the report of the United States Commissioner of Education for 1909. These schools enroll 9,775 boys and 13,734 girls of elementary grades, 7,751 boys and 9,258 girls of secondary grade, and 2,885 men and 1,300 women of collegiate grade.[1]

Leaders in Training

In other words, there were in process of training for leadership in the ministry, teaching and the professions only 2,885 men in the year 1909. This little handful of men—not so many as the number of colored teachers in the single State of Georgia—are to be the leaders of 9,000,000 colored people. Surely this is not an overcrowding in the realm of trained leadership.

Work for 33 Colleges and their Graduates

Professor DuBois, in the report of the Atlanta University Conference for 1902, tabulates thirty-

---

[1] "Report of U. S. Commissioner of Education," 1909.

three colleges that he thinks should really bear that title. From these colleges up to 1899 there have been graduated 2,008 negroes. From the Northern universities there have been graduated several hundred more (400?), so that from all sources Professor DuBois estimates there are probably 2,500 negro graduates in America. Of this number probably 80 per cent. are at work in the South. In order to find out what these college graduates do an investigation was undertaken by Atlanta University. Letters were written to all the 2,500 college-bred negroes who could be located, asking their occupation, etc. 1,312 sent replies. Of this number 701 or 53 per cent. were teachers, 221 or 17 per cent. were preachers, 83 or 6.3 per cent. were physicians, 53 or 4 per cent. were in Civil Service work, and the remainder were in business, farming, secretarial positions, etc. [1] Of the efficiency of these graduates and of the moral worth, Booker T. Washington writes: "Not a single graduate of the Hampton Institute or of the Tuskegee Institute can be found to-day in any jail or State penitentiary. After making careful inquiry, I cannot find a half-dozen cases of a man or a woman who has completed a full course of education in any of our reputable institutions like Hampton, Tuskegee, Fisk or Atlanta who are in prisons. The records of the South show that 90 per cent. of the colored people in prisons are without knowledge of trades, and 61 per cent. are illiterate." [2]

This is surely a splendid showing, and should

---

[1] Atlanta University Publication, No. 5, *passim.*
[2] "Working with Hands," p. 235.

put our minds at ease on this much-mooted question of the higher education of the negro.

Recommendations of Southern Educational Association

That the education of the negro is not a failure is well indicated by the resolutions adopted by the Southern Educational Association at its meeting in 1907:

"We endorse the accepted policy of the States of the South in providing educational facilities for the youth of the negro race, believing that whatever the ultimate solution of this grievous problem may be, education must be an important factor in that solution."

"We believe that the education of the negro in the elementary branches of education should be made thorough, and should include specific instruction in hygiene and home sanitation, for the better protection of both races."

"We believe that in the secondary education of negro youth, emphasis should be placed upon agriculture and the industrial occupations, including nurse training, domestic science, and home economics."

"We believe that for practical, economical and psychological reasons negro teachers should be provided for negro schools."

"We advise instruction in normal schools and normal institutions by white teachers, whenever possible, and closer supervision of courses of study and methods of teaching in negro normal schools by the State Department of Education."

"We recommend that in urban and rural negro schools there should be closer and more thorough

supervision, not only by city and county super-
intendents, but also by directors of music, draw-
ing, manual training, and other special topics."

"We urge upon school authorities everywhere
the importance of adequate buildings, comfort-
able seating, and sanitary accommodations for
negro youth."

"We deplore the isolation of many negro
schools, established through motives of philanthropy, from the life and the sympathies of the
communities in which they are located. We
recommend the supervision of all such schools
by the State, and urge that their work and their
methods be adjusted to the civilization in which
they exist, in order that the maximum good of
the race and of the community may be thereby
attained."

"On account of economics and psychological
difference in the two races, we believe that there
should be a difference in courses of study and
methods of teaching, and that there should be
such an adjustment of school curricula as shall
meet the evident needs of negro youth."

"We insist upon such an equitable distribution
of the school funds that all the youth of the
negro race shall have at least an opportunity to
receive the elementary education provided by the
State, and in the administration of State laws,
and in the execution of this educational policy, we
urge patience, tolerance and justice."

Education vs. Ignorance

It has never been found in all the world that a
sane and thorough intellectual equipment has

been detrimental to morals or to industrial efficiency.   The negro is no exception to this rule.   It
is not the educated negro that fills our penitentiary and jails, works in our chain gangs and fills
our poor-houses.   These places are given over
to the ignorant and depraved.   It is not the educated negro that makes up our idle and vagrant
class, that commits our murders and despoils
our women.   Here, again, it is the illiterate and
degraded negro.   The trained negro lives in a
better home, wears better clothes, eats better
food, does more efficient work, creates more
wealth, rears his children more decently, makes a
more decent citizen, and in times of race friction
is always to be found on the side of law and
order.   These things seem to be worthy fruits,
and whatever system produces them should have
our approval.   If we are to be fair to ourselves,
fair to the section in which we live, and fair to
the negro race, we must see that a common school
education is provided for all, that industrial training is given to the majority, and that a more
thorough and complete training shall be given to
the capable few who are to become the leaders of
this race.

V

THE RELIGIOUS LIFE OF THE NEGRO

RELIGION

I am no priest of crooks nor creeds,
For human wants and human needs
Are more to me than prophets' deeds;
And human tears and human cares
Affect me more than human prayers.

Go, cease your wail, lugubrious saint!
You fret high Heaven with your plaint.
Is this the "Christian's joy" you paint?
Is this the Christian's boasted bliss?
Avails your faith no more than this?

Take up your arms, come out with me,
Let Heav'n alone; humanity
Needs more and Heaven less from thee.
With pity for mankind look 'round;
Help them to rise—and Heaven is found.

—PAUL LAURENCE DUNBAR.

THE RELIGIOUS LIFE OF THE NEGRO

Religious Index

One index of the life of a people is its religion. Find the context of that term and you have found the key to the civilization or the savagery of a people, the key to its progress or its stagnation. Not only the content of a religion but the attitude of a people toward that religion are topics of supreme importance in a discussion such as this.

What is Religion

Professor Rhys-Davids contends that religion includes three conceptions, "first, beliefs as to internal and external mysteries (souls and gods)—second, the mental attitudes induced by these beliefs, thirdly, the actions and conduct dependent upon both." [1]

Professor Jevons would define religion as "man's consciousness of a supernatural spirit (or spirits) having affinity with his own spirit and having power over him." [2] Dr. Tiele says: "The origin of religion consists in the fact that man *has* the Infinite within him even before he is himself

---

[1] "Buddhism: American Lectures," p. 4.
[2] Introduction to the "History of Religion," p. 15.

conscious of it, and whether he recognizes it or not."[1]

Perhaps we may define religion as man's consciousness of a higher but kindred being with whom he desires and ought to live on terms of truest fellowship. If such be in any sense a true definition of religion, it will be readily seen that such consciousness must have deep meaning for every nation as well as for every individual.

Negro Ancestry

In order that we may understand the religion of the present negro, we must take a look at his religious life in his fatherland. According to Mr. Dowd[2] the races of Africa fall under five divisions. First, the Negritos, dwelling in the lowlands of the central equatorial region; second, the Negritians, occupying the territory of the Sudan; third, the Fellatahs, scattered among the Negritians of Central Sudan; fourth, the Bantus, occupying almost all the Western portion of the continent, south of the fourth degree of north latitude; and fifth, the Gallas, occupying the southeastern portion of Africa. It was from the fourth division, the Bantus, that most of the slaves were brought to America, and it is among these same tribes that the atrocities of the rubber and ivory trade have recently been perpetrated.

God's Self-Revelation

It is generally agreed now by anthropologists, I believe, that there are no races, however rude,

[1] "Elements of the Science of Religion," Vol. 2, p. 30.
[2] "The Negro Races," p. 11.

that are destitute of all idea of religion.[1] It is
further agreed, I believe, by most Christian think-
ers that God has always been trying and still is
trying to make Himself known to all men. That
this revelation is not equally clear and without
admixture for all men need not cause surprise,
for the content of a message is not determined
alone by the speaker, but by the varying capaci-
ties and degrees of attention on the part of the
listeners. That the Bantu tribes have some conception of God—however crude it may seem—
is not doubted by those that have worked among
them longest and known them best.

"Standing in the village street, surrounded by
a company whom their chief has graciously sum-
moned at my request, I do not need to begin by
telling them that there is a God. Looking on that
motley assembly of villagers—the bold, gaunt
cannibal with his armament of gun, spear, and
dagger; the artisan with rude adz in hand, or
hands soiled at the antique bellows of the village
smithy; women who have hastened from their
kitchen fire with hands white with the manioc
dough or still grasping the partly scaled fish—
I have yet to be asked, 'Who is God?' "[2]

"The belief in one great Supreme Being is universal. Nor is this idea held imperfectly or ob-
scurely developed in their minds. The impression
is so deeply engraved upon their moral and mental nature that any system of Atheism strikes

---

[1] Jevons' "Introduction to the History of Religion,"
p. 7.
[2] "Fetichism in West Africa," Nassau, p. 36.

them as too absurd and preposterous to require a denial."[1]

Debased Conception of God

But, of course, this conception of God is much debased and mixed with many superstitions. They do not think of God as a father who loves and cares for his children, but as a vague being responsible for man's existence, but caring little for man's destiny. "The prevailing notion seems to be that God, after having made the world and filled it with inhabitants, retired to some remote corner of the universe, and has allowed the affairs of the world to come under the control of evil spirits; and hence the only religious worship that is ever performed is directed to these spirits, the object of which is to court their favor, or ward off the evil effects of their displeasure."[2]

Spirits

The spirits are of three classes as to origin. First, those existing from eternity—those conterminous with the Supreme being — Paia-Njambi; second, those created by the Supreme Being; third, the souls of dead human beings. These spirits fill the air and inhabit the rocks, the caverns, the trees and even take up their abode in wild animals. Graveyards are their favorite abiding places, hence every native stands in fear of such grounds.

[1] Wilson's "Western Africa," p. 39.
[2] *Idem*, p. 39.

Origin of Belief in Spirits

The original conception of spirits probably arose from two sources. First, all savages believe that not only plants and animals have spirits but also inanimate things. Whatever moves has life—has a spirit. The stream as it runs and sings, the lightning as it flashes or strikes, the flame as it flickers or consumes the wood are all supposed to be alive. Not only so, but the rock against which man falls and it cuts him, the tree which seems to spring of itself out of the ground, and numerous other objects have life within them. Thus animism—the imputing of spirits to objects of nature—has its rise, and from this it is a short step to the fear and worship of spirits.

Secondly, the idea of spirits arises from man's experiences in dreams. These experiences to the savage are as real as any waking experience. While he sleeps his spirit wanders—it meets the spirits of friends and they recognize each other; when he wakes he is perfectly sure that he has seen and talked with his friend. But he is told that his body has been in his bed—well, then, his spirit has been journeying at will. When he wakes—this is just the return of his spirit to his body. Hence death is simply a continued sleep, where the spirit refuses to return to its body. When a man dies, therefore, his spirit is set wandering, having power to help or harm where it pleases. His spirit may take up its abode in an animal and return to vex the life of his enemies or even his own family. Dr. Nassau tells us of a native who refused to kill an ele-

phant that was ravaging his crop, because he
thought his dead father's spirit had taken up its
abode in that particular animal.

Character of Spirits

The character of these disembodied spirits is
the same as the characters of the living men.
They are benevolent or malevolent, full of kind-
ness or full of hatred, in accordance with their
former existence. If they have been slighted
while in their embodied form, they may come
back to take revenge on their enemies. The fact
that these spirits have not the encumbrance of
a body may make them ten times more powerful
than any living man, and the further fact that
they can act without detection throws about the
life of the native African a constant dread and
fear which is almost paralyzing.

Origin of Magic Witch Doctors

The one recourse of the savage is to placate
these spirits, winning their favor and warding
off their anger. This gives rise to a complicated
system of magic. In order to protect himself
against the anger of these spirits, the native
employs the services of the witch doctor. This
witch doctor or medicine man is supposed to have
great power over evil spirits. They have power
to condemn to death any person suspected of
causing death; they are supposed to be able to
drive out the spirits that cause sickness; they
may call back the spirits of those near unto
death—for all of which services they demand
great respect and large fees.

Meaning of Fetiches

One of the chief methods of work of the medicine man or witch doctor is the preparation and use of fetiches. A fetich is any rag, string, stone, shell, tooth, piece of wood or what not, into which a magic doctor has coaxed a spirit to take up its abode, or into which a spirit has voluntarily entered. The material in itself is not sacred, but the fact that a spirit dwells in it gives it power to ward off sickness or defend one against his enemies. If the spirit leaves the fetich then the wood or stone is cast away and another is found. "He addresses his prayer to it and extols its virtues; but should his enterprise not prosper he will cast his deity aside as useless, and cease to worship it; he will address it with torrents of abuse, and will even beat it, to make it serve him better. It is a deity at his disposal, to serve in the accomplishment of his desires; the individual keeps gods of his own to help him in his undertakings." [1]

White and Black Art

So long as these fetiches are used simply for protection the owner is a practicer of white art, but, when they are used to injure others or force others to do certain things pleasing to the owner of the fetich, their possessor is said to practice black art. It is this latter that keeps the African native in constant fear. At any hour his enemy may by witchcraft destroy his property, rob him of his friends or take his life. All that an enemy has to do is to get some of his

[1] "History of Religion." p. 32. Menzies.

victim's hair, his nails, or water in which he has bathed, and have a witch doctor make a concoction which, buried in front of the victim's door or secretly hung in his room, will bring sure death. If the man dies, this black art has worked; if he fails to die, then he himself has a fetich stronger than the spirit that was trying to induce his death. In this murderous superstition the natives have absolute confidence.

Religious Constituents

These, then, are the constituents of the African religion: A God who created man and is supreme, but who has gone away into the corner of the universe and is no longer interested in his creation; an infinite host of spirits, good and bad, which hold the destinies of men in their hands and whose favor must, therefore, be won; witch doctors and medicine men who conjure with the spirits and keep the people in constant awe; fetiches which are the habitats of spirits used for protection; and the practice of black art with all of its murderous motives and deeds. Of course, there are elements of moral power in this religion, but so much is it degraded that one almost wonders if God has been able to reveal himself in the smallest degree to these people.

Religion of the Slave

When the Bantu slave was brought to America he brought with him all the superstitions, all the wild savagery of his religion. One does not need to go far to find that this religion still has its remnants in the life of the negro race of

to-day. In particular the fetich held sway among these benighted people—as is still exemplified in the carrying of the rabbit foot and other relics for the sake of warding off evil. "Not only did this religion of the fetich endure under slavery, it grew. It was a secret religion that lurked thinly covered in slavery days, and that lurks to-day beneath the negro's Christian profession as a white art, and among non-professors as a black art; a memory of the revenges of his African ancestors." [1] Thousands of negroes still believe implicitly in hoodoos, spirits, witchcraft, ghosts. In the city of Nashville, some years ago, a group of medical students went out to "snatch" a body for dissecting purposes. They were piloted by a negro man who betrayed them into the hands of a band of armed negroes. In the dark of the night the armed negroes shot into the party and accidentally killed the negro pilot. Since that time the house which he then occupied has not been used. No negro will rent it for fear of being troubled by the spirit of the dead man who was killed because of treachery. A negro that has had considerable schooling and has had employment among white people for years told me that the spirit of this man could be heard every night moaning and crying in the house where he had formerly lived. As a test I offered this negro five dollars to go with me at midnight into this house, which he refused, saying he would not go for five hundred. This seems to me purely a survival of the old African spirit belief. Hoodoo or Voodoo (French Creole

[1] "Fetichism in West Africa. p. 274. Nassau.

Vaudois—the witchcraft of the Waldensians) is no more nor less than the survival of the black art, against which a fetich or charm must be carried.

"And you's got a rabbit foot to drive away the Hoodoo!"

It is not unlikely that the stories of Uncle Remus are direct descendants of the folk tales which lived centuries ago in Africa. In fact, many of the superstitions of the uneducated negro of to-day can be traced directly back to the African home of the slave.

Tenacity of Religious Tradition

Religious tradition outlives all others, and may manifest itself long after its origin or meaning is forgotten. We need not be surprised, therefore, if we find the religious life of the American negro filled with superstition and less related to morals than our own ethical sense would demand. We must remember that New England did not throw off her witchcraft for many years and not all the white people of the South are free from belief in a hoodoo.

Grades of Religious Life

It must be understood that negro religious life, like any other religious life, varies widely. There are many well educated and cultured negroes who have moved far away from all the superstitions, and in whose lives their religion is a vital moral force. Of these we will speak more at length under religious development. We are

here concerned about the elemental types of negro religion.

Characterization of Negro Religion

From what has preceded we are prepared to
believe that the religion of the masses may be
characterized as partly superstitious, largely
emotional, and in an alarmingly small degree
ethical. Perhaps enough has been said to indicate the bearing of superstition upon religion.
The negro has a tropical imagination which
revels in the strange, mysterious or supernatural,
and this type of mind, touched with a deep emotionalism and augmented by ignorance, may easily
give rise to the most grotesque types of religious
belief.

Emotional Element

The emotionalism of the negro religion—I
mean the religion of the great masses who are
ignorant—is well known to every Southern man.
I have visited negro churches where the sermon
could scarcely be called more than a wild chant
or incantation. The high shrieking voice of the
preacher as he calls over and over again the
refrain of his text in dull monotony—is inter-
rupted continually by the heavy groans and occasionally by the weird cry of a happy "mourner."
Professor DuBois describes his first negro
camp meeting as follows: "A sort of sup-
pressed terror hung in the air, and seemed to
seize us—a pythian madness, a demoniac possession, that lent terrible reality to song and
words. The black and massive form of the

preacher swayed and quivered as the words crowded to his lips and flew at us in singular eloquence. The people moaned and fluttered, and then the gaunt-cheeked brown woman beside me suddenly leaped straight into the air and shrieked like a lost soul, while round about came wail and groan and outcry and a scene of human passion such as I had never before conceived." [1]

Mr. L. C. Perry, in a sociological study of the negro, printed in the Vanderbilt University Quarterly, April, 1904, gives the following account of a service in one of the cruder churches of Nashville: "A very warm evening. Every seat in the house packed and most of the standing room occupied. Two stoves nearly red hot and the door kept tightly shut. Text: 'And the Lord spoke to Daniel in the valley of dry bones, saying, Rise ye up and meet me.' The sermon began something like this: 'Brethren and sisters, I started out early one morning, a long time ago, and knew not witherward I was going for the Lord was leading of me in ways unbeknownst to me, henceward I went on and on till finally when the day got hot I came down into the valley of Jehosaphat. And as I went down the slippery walls of that slimy valley my weary feet slided over rottening bones of many hell-parched sinners. I fell not, though the valley was full of pits and horrible falls; I fell not, for a band of holy angels were rustling their wings around me to bear me upward and onward to meet my God, and they bore me on and I came to my Lord, and he was——' Here followed a descrip-

[1] "Souls of Black Folk," p. 190.

tion of his meeting the Lord; but what he said could not be understood, for his voice was drowned by the shouts of twenty-five or more people. 'Then my Lord told me to come here to Nashville, to Kayne Avenue, and preach to his chosen lambs for to rise up and meet their God——' Then much more shouting, which, in fact, never entirely died out at any time, and only at intervals allowed the speaker to be heard. The harangue lasted in this strain for an hour and a half without touching the ground."

Negro Prayers

"The prayers are often more offensive than the sermon. Bass Street Church, first Sunday evening in May. A very small house, only forty-five present, and six of them preachers. The pastor called on one of the young preachers to pray. He prayed eleven minutes, and, after the first few sentences, fell into a perfectly uniform mode of expression and montonous chant. His sentences were all alike, with the exception of only one clause in each. "O! Lord, my God, wilt thou be so good and so kind and so merciful as to condescend as to bless us? O! Lord, my God, wilt thou be so good and so kind and so merciful as to condescend as to bless our little children?" And on and on with the use of this same expression till a blessing had been invoked on everything imaginable, from the stars in heaven even to the pavements of the streets, while at the same time another preacher was keeping up a symmetrical chant of response: "O! yes, Lord grant it; O! do Lord, amen and

amen. O! yes, Lord grant it; O! do Lord, amen
and amen." And a layman, presumably so from
his position out in the congregation, also kept a
chant going; but he uttered no word that could
be distinguished, though at certain evenly measured intervals his voice rose very high. And
then, besides all of this, there was another man
whose action is hard to describe or name. He was
perfectly quiet except at well-measured points
in the prayer, about twenty seconds apart, when
he raised a hideous, indescribable snort, more
like the sound of an animal than a human being.
The effect of all this was weird, and one often
had to pull himself together to realize that he
was still in Nashville and had not been suddenly
transported to Africa."

Lack of Ethical Content

Naturally, a superstitious and emotional religion does not do much to affect the standard of
morals. It is not simply a discrepancy between
creed and practice, as Kelly Miller puts it, for
that is found often among whites, but, with the
mass of the negroes, religion is lacking both
in ethical creed and ethical practice. Religion
is a thing to die by and not to live by. It
has reference to states of ecstacy but little to
do with a man's state of morals. A negro man
of much more than average sense—one whom I
have known for years and have never known him
to be dishonest or untruthful—said to me about
his preacher lately: "He's a purty good lecturer,
but he can't preach much." When I questioned
him I found he meant that his preacher was good

at making appeals for honesty, purity, sobriety, etc., but he did not use much "gravy" as they call the sing-song chant and hysterical oratory. A teacher in a negro college told me once that many of their graduates went out with the idea of preaching a real gospel of moral life, but the pressure from the congregations they served was so great that they frequently had to abandon their gospel and more and more fall into the habit of putting on the "rousements."

Rev. W. H. Holloway's Testimony

Rev. W. H. Holloway, a graduate of Talladega College, a Congregational minister in charge of a colored church in Thomas County, Ga., in a study of the negro church in that county, writes as follows:

"The supreme element in the old system was emotionalism, and while we hate to confess it truth demands that we affirm it as the predominating element to-day. The church which does not have its shouting, the church which does not measure the abilities of a preacher by the 'rousement' of his sermons, and, indeed, which does not tacitly demand of its minister the shout-producing discourse, is an exception to the rule. This is true of the towns as well as the country. Of course, we all understand that it has always occupied first place in the worship of the negro church; it is a heritage of the past. In the absence of clearly defined doctrines, the great shout, accompanied with weird cries and shrieks and contortions and followed by a multivaried 'experience' which takes the candidate through the

most heart-rending scenes—this to-day in Thomas
County is accepted by the majority of the churches
as unmistakable evidence of regeneration."

I spoke some time since at a negro university
on sins of men and after the address the negro
physician, himself a Christian man, told me that
ninety-eight per cent. was too low an estimate
for the negro men who live or have lived impure
lives, and yet forty-eight per cent. of them are
church members. This divorcement of religion
and morals is perhaps the most serious phase of
the negro problem.

Encouragement in Spite of this Picture

I am well aware that I have not drawn a
bright picture. A religion divorced from morals,
with intense emotionalism and with crudest superstitions is not altogether a hopeful factor in
developing a race. One does not like to write
such a statement but one must be true to facts.
And yet all is not hopeless. There is a brighter
side to the picture. It is surely hopeful that
such a large proportion of the negroes are religious, that the religious hunger is planted deep
in their nature. When there is a hungering and
thirsting, there is a chance that men may be
filled. This very fact of the religious nature of the
negro gives the surest indication that he can be
helped, that he can be moralized, that he can be
made into a true citizen. We only need to help
him purify his ideas of religion, and that is never
so difficult a task as to create a capacity for religious truth.

A Progressive Minority

There is a second sign of hope in the fact that

there is a growing minority of the race with a religion of moral content. I heard a sermon by a negro preacher recently on the text: "I am the way, the truth and the life." It was clear, logical and full of practical suggestion. It is sheer pessimism, if not ignorant prejudice, or perhaps it is both, to say that religion with all negroes is divorced from morality. I know negroes—even uneducated negroes—whose religion means honesty, truthfulness, and purity. I know negroes of culture with whom religion has as much of content as it has for the cultured white man. This is the foundation for a real hope. If a minority has moved up into a realm of genuine religion, then the mass, with sufficient cultivation and care, may be brought into the same realm. If any considerable minority is capable of knowing and practicing genuine religious truth, there is possibility of redeeming the whole race from its ignorance, its superstition and its immorality. If anyone doubts that there is such a minority the one way to convince himself is to visit some of the best negro churches and see for himself. Let him come to know some of the best negroes and watch their conduct and even the most skeptical will be convinced.

These two pictures put on every man who reads an obligation. If there is a minority with a real religion of moral and spiritual content, and if there is a great mass with a religion of low moral and low spiritual content, then it is our duty as enlightened Christian men to give to this second class a vital Gospel. [1]

---

[1] *Cf.* Chapter I.

The Missionary Appeal

The greatest appeal that a missionary from the heart of Africa, or of China, or of India, can make is this: "The people are in ignorance, they are in sin, their religions are full of errors, they do not know our God—we have a real gospel of life and we must take it to them, for they are capable of receiving and are glad to hear." This is precisely the appeal that can be made on behalf of the lower half of the negroes at our very doors. It is splendid to have a missionary spirit, but God knows no home or foreign lands—he simply knows that a black man in America may be as needy as a black man in Africa and His Gospel will help both alike.

The Negro Church

The embodied expression of religion is the Church and no discussion of negro religion would be complete without some word about church life. In the early days of slavery in America there was great question as to whether slaves should be allowed to receive baptism or to join the church, lest such action might make them free. It always seemed somewhat incongruous for a man who was a Christian and a church member to be a slave. However, Virginia, in 1667, passed a law that "Baptism doth not alter the condition of the person as to his bondage or freedom, in order that divers masters freed from this doubt may more carefully endeavor the propagation of Christianity." [1] North Carolina passed a similar law in 1670 and so the propagation of Christianity among slaves went on.

[1] "The Negro Church," p. 8.

The Church in Slave Days

Most of the converted slaves belonged to the white churches since it was feared that separate churches would give too great opportunity for the stirring up of discontent and strife. Indeed, a number of the States went so far as to make it a finable offense for any master to allow his slaves to build or worship in a separate church. However, the records show that "various masters had their own ministers whom they paid to instruct their slaves in religious matters."

Early Work. Moravians

The Moravians early began a missionary work among the negroes. As early as 1735 missionaries were sent into South Carolina and Georgia to preach the gospel. Work was also undertaken among the negroes of Philadelphia.

Presbyterians

The Presbyterians, under the leadership of Rev. Samuel Davis, began work in Virginia before the middle of the eighteenth century. In 1755 Dr. Davis writes: "A considerable number of them had been baptized, after a proper time for instruction, having given creditable evidence not only of their acquaintance with the important doctrines of the Christian religion, but also a deep sense of them in their minds, attested by a life of strict piety and holiness."[1]

Methodists

In 1776 the Methodists began work in Virginia and in the great revivals that followed

---

[1] "The Negro Church," p. 17.

many negroes, along with the whites, were converted. The minutes of the Methodist Conference for 1786 show a membership of 18,791
whites and 1890 colored. In 1791, there were
12,884 colored members reported; in 1792, there
were 13,871; in 1793, there were 16,227; in 1794,
there were 13,814; in 1795, 12,179. The decrease
in numbers is probably due to the great revivals
in the Baptist Church during the last two years
mentioned, and the preaching of colored ministers
which drew many members from other churches
into the Baptist fold. According to the order
of the conference of 1790 the Bishops, elders
and preachers were to appoint leaders for schools
to be taught on Sundays from 6:00 to 10:00 A.M.
and from 2:00 to 6:00 P.M., in which all colored
children who desired might be taught to read
the Bible.

Baptists

Between 1785 and 1792 during the great Baptist revivals many negroes were converted and
brought into the Baptist Church. In 1792 the
first colored Baptist church was built in the city
of Charleston, the city contributing the lot. This
denomination had had negro preachers for twenty
years prior to this time.

Awakening of 1830

About 1830 there was a great revival of interest among all the churches of the South in
the evangelization of the slaves. "A reaction
set in about 1835, and the Methodists and Baptists especially were active among the slaves.

A minister in Mississippi testified that he had charge of the negroes of five plantations and three hundred slaves; another in Georgia visited eighteen plantations every two weeks. 'Two owners have built three good churches at their own expense, all framed, 290 members have been added, and about 400 children are instructed.' Another traveling minister declared, in 1841, that in many places like Baltimore, Alexandria, and Charleston, the negroes had large spacious churches, and he thinks there were 500,000 negro church members at the time." [1] Whether this is an overestimation or not we cannot determine, but it indicates that the Southern churches and the owners of slaves were far from unmindful of their duty to look after the moral life of the slaves.

In 1860, according to Bishop McTyiere, the number of slaves that were members of the Southern conferences of the Methodist Episcopal Church were 207,000. This church alone through its conference in the Southern States contributed between the years of 1844 and 1860, inclusive, $1,320,778.03 for the evangelization of the slaves. In the year 1861 this church alone had 327 missionaries among the negroes and spent $86,359.20. [2]

Organization of Separate Negro Churches

The African Methodist Episcopal Church was organized in 1816 at Baltimore by the withdrawal of a number of negro members from the Metho-

---

[1] "The Negro Church," p. 28.
[2] "Gospel Among the Slaves." p. 318. Harrison & Barnes.

dist Episcopal Church. Rev. Richard Allen was elected their first Bishop by this organizing conference. This church has now about half a million members and nearly three thousand organized churches.

Another branch from the Methodist Episcopal Church is the African Methodist Episcopal Zion organized in 1811. It now has nearly four hundred thousand adherents.

The Colored Methodist Episcopal is a branch of the Methodist Episcopal Church South and was organized in 1870. It now has a membership approximating one hundred and fifty thousand.

The Cumberland Presbyterian Church (colored) was organized in 1869, at Murfreesboro, Tennessee. It has fifteen thousand members and property valued at two hundred thousand dollars ($200,000).

Regular Baptists (colored) constitute the largest single communion of negroes. The first Colored Baptist Convention was organized in North Carolina, 1866. They now have a million and a half members and property valued at ten millions of dollars.

Summary of Negro Churches

The census of 1890 gives the total number of members or communicants as 2,673,977 and the total property valuation at $26,626,448. It seems likely that the 1910 census will give a total membership of between four and four and a half millions. Mr. John Wesley Gilbert, of the Colored Methodist Episcopal Church, estimates that property valuation now aggregates forty millions of dollars. Here is a powerful organization. What is its strength and what are its weaknesses?

Inclusive Character of Negro Church Its First Source of Strength

The first element of the strength of the Negro Church lies in its all-inclusive character. It is not simply the place for worship, it is also the social center of the race, the place of amusement and to an extent the place for gathering information. The negro church has been called the first distinctively negro American social institution. During slave days the home was not a place of much social power. While there were many masters who did what they could to give their slaves something of home life, the conditions were such and the past history of the slave was such that little could be effected. It easily came about, therefore, that the church stood for whatever of social ideals the negro had. After the war, the home life of the negro improved very slowly and even to this day there is really no home life for great masses of negroes. The church, therefore, still holds its sway as a powerful social factor.

The Church and Amusement

Likewise the church is the center of amusement. In few cities do the negroes have any theaters, amusement halls, etc. Hence the church has had to step in and become the center of amusement. Here the debating club holds sway; here in later days the moving picture is seen. The fact that the church is the center of

amusements has put a severe ban on many forms
of pleasure. There is practically no outdoor
amusement for the negro, save peeping over the
fence to see a white ball game, or in the country
or small town district having a country "break
down." The fact that the negro church has
been the center both of the social life and of the
pleasure life of the negro has given to it a very
firm hold on the negro race.

Material Equipment

A second fact of real importance is the material equipment of the negro church. While
many of the buildings are poor and uninviting,
it must be acknowledged that the race has done
splendidly to erect buildings aggregating in cost
$40,000,000. This is no small asset for the power
of the church.

Breadth of Influence

Another strength of the church lies in the fact
that it reaches almost the whole community instead of just a fraction of the community as is
the case of the white church. It is estimated that
forty-eight per cent. of the negroes are church
members and many more are adherents and regular attendants. However poor the gospel that
is preached, there is power for good in the fact
that the vast majority of the race has respect for
the church and attend its services.

Educated Ministers

Possibly the most important asset of the negro
church lies in its increasing number of educated

ministers. On the darker side of the question we must say a word later, but it is only fair to say here that the standard is certainly rising. In the cities where the problems are more difficult there is an increasing number of pastors that are college and seminary graduates. In such churches the service is orderly, the sermons are wholesome, logical and practical. This is perhaps the most encouraging sign of the whole negro problem to-day.

Uneducated Ministry a Weakness

With all of these elements of strength there are also not a few weaknesses in the negro church. The first of these is the other side of our last sentence—the low average intelligence and morality of the negro ministry. Here, lest we shall be unfair in our judgment, let a negro minister speak:

Dougherty County, Georgia

"We have been able to learn of about 120 preachers in the county. Of this number fully seventy-five are either ordained or licensed. The most of their names appear in the minutes of the various denominations. Now this number may be almost doubled if we search for all those who call themselves preachers and fill the function of interpreters of the Word of God. This number moulds as great a sentiment for or against the church as those who hold license."

"You will get some idea of the vast host who belong to this class when I tell you that the records of the last conference of the Southwest

Georgia District of the African Methodist Episcopal Church show that there were forty-three applicants for admission to the conference. Note that this is only one of the four or five conferences of this church in the State. Be it said, to the lasting credit of the conference, that it in unmistakable terms put the stamp of condemnation upon the presumption of about thirty-five of them and sent them back to their homes disappointed men. And yet, while it sent them back home unadmitted, it did not make them less determined to preach, for in their several communities you will find them still exercising themselves in the holy calling." [1]

Character of Ministers

In an investigation made by Atlanta University concerning the character of the negro ministry, two hundred negro laymen were asked their opinion of the moral character of negro preachers. It is remarkable that only thirty-seven gave decided answers of approval. All the others made some qualifications. Among faults mentioned by these negro laymen were selfishness, deceptiveness, love for money, sexual impurity, dogmatism, laziness, ignorance, etc. It cannot be doubted that these adjectives carry all too large a truth. In this connection also may be mentioned again the type of preaching done by many of these ministers. It is highly emotional and lacking in any practical moral message.

[1] Rev. W. H. Holloway. Study of Thomas County, Ga. "The Negro Church," p. 61.

Church Splits

Another weakness of the church lies in its spirit of rivalry and dissensions. None of the churches seem so far to have devised a system of government that will cement its members into strong, compact organizations. In most cases organization counts for little, personal prejudice counts for much. If debate arises in the church over the ability of a preacher, one wing will pull off and establish a new church. Hence it arises that many of the negro churches are family churches, being the relatives and friends of some dissenting pastor who organized the new church. Rev. W. H. Holloway declares that of the ninety-eight churches in Thomas County, Georgia, about half of them originated out of a church split. "I know of no rural churches in Thomas County whose inception had the careful nursing of an educated, cultured leader. The largest churches and the biggest preachers in Thomas County do little home missionary work and organize no new churches." [1] This means that there are twice as many church organizations as there should be, there are too many church buildings, that congregations are too small, and hence salaries paid to ministers cannot be large enough to secure competent men.

In going over the list of fifty-four churches in the City of Atlanta, I find seventeen churches with less than one hundred members, the average membership of these seventeen being thirty. Only eight of the fifty-four had more than two hundred, and only four had more than three hun-

[1] "The Negro Church," p. 57.

dred members. Eleven of these Atlanta churches are the outgrowth of church splits.

In the City of Nashville there are fifty-two negro churches, the average membership of which is two hundred and seven, while the average in the white churches is nearly twice as great, three hundred and ninety. There are seventeen negro churches in Nashville with less than one hundred members each. This condition at once accounts for poor church buildings and the low grade of ministers.

Loose Business Methods

Lack of business methods is another weakness of the negro church. In this the negro church has no monopoly, as, indeed, it has not in any of the other weaknesses mentioned. All of these weaknesses are simply more marked in the negro than in the white church. Of one hundred and sixty-five negro laymen asked concerning the progress of the negro church, thirty-five answered decidedly that its financial management was very bad. Again, let a negro minister speak for us on this question:

"Another condition which gives rise to our assertion that the church is not exercising its highest moral influence, is seen in its lax business methods. Let us give one example, which we dare assert is true of nine-tenths of the churches in Thomas County, and in the South: A contract is made with every incoming minister. They promise him a stipulated sum for his year's service, and when the year ends he goes to conference with only about two-thirds of the pledge fulfilled. If he is sent back to the same field, the second year finds the church still deeper on the debit side of the ledger. If he is sent to another field the debt is considered settled, a new contract is made with the new preacher, and the same form is gone through." [1]

Danger of Losing Its Aim

Lastly, we must mention the fact that the non-essentials of the church are in danger of absorbing its whole life to the exclusion of its real functions of religious teaching. The numerous church socials, the multitudinous societies, the prominence given to certain rites and ceremonies, fill the life of the average church member to a dangerous extent. The church is primarily a place for worship, for religious instruction, and for religious fellowship and service. When it loses its distinctively religious character it is in danger of losing its power.

The Appeal of Facts

Here, then, is a problem of no small concern to every Southern man. We live in a section of the country where eight million colored people live. Whatever affects the lives of these people affects our lives. The colored man is a decidedly religious being, but if his religion is not worthy it will degrade rather than elevate him. The church which fosters his religion is torn with internal dissensions which weaken its power and dissipate its energies; its ministers are all too frequently ignorant, lazy and immoral; its gos-

---

[1] "The Negro Church," p. 60.

pel is in many cases an emotional hysteria, with little reference to morals; and the majority of white men are either ignorant or indifferent to these facts. Shall we, as southern college men, not be statesmen-like enough to see the importance of this present situation, and lend our help in meeting the present needs? And the conditions are by no means hopeless. The negro is teachable, he is deeply religious, he looks to the white man for counsel, he will welcome aid from any college man—and, what is best of all, he is making substantial progress in higher religious ideals.

VI

WHAT CAN WE DO?

RIGHT'S SECURITY

What if the wind do howl without,
And turn the creaking weather-vane;
What if the arrows of the rain
Do beat against the window-pane?
Art thou not armored strong and fast
Against the sallies of the blast?
Art thou not sheltered safe and well
Against the flood's insistent swell?

What boots it, that thou stand'st alone,
And laughest in the battle's face
When all the weak have fled the place
And let their feet and fears keep pace?
Thou wavest still thine ensign high,
And shouted thy loud battle-cry;
Higher than e'er the tempest roared,
It cleaves the silence like a sword.

Right arms and armors, too, that man
Who will not compromise with wrong;
Though single, he must front the throng,
And wage the battle hard and long.
Minorities, since time began,
Have shown the better side of man;
And often in the lists of time
One man has made a cause sublime!

—Paul Laurence Dunbar.

VI

WHAT CAN WE DO?

Present Social Awakening

Ours may be characterized as a sociological age. Men are thinking to-day in terms of social life. It would be safe to say that more books dealing with social questions have come from the press within the last twenty-five years than in all the previous centuries of the world's history. There is a widespread awakening to the facts of all humanity and a consequent interest in them. One would scarcely dare to say that this is a wholly modern movement, for it has its roots deep in the soil of the past, but its flower can hardly be said to have burst into bloom until this present generation.

World Unity

At least three elements—each of which have had much accentuation during the last decade—have entered into this growing social consciousness. First of these may be mentioned the principle of a spiritual monism. Slowly, but surely, philosophy has been moving away from the various forms of dualism, until it now proclaims a unifying element in the universe, into which all forces and all beings are caught up and knit into one complete whole. Behind the forces of nature there is a supreme force; behind the lives of the universe, there is a supreme life; and these blend into a complete and perfect personality, whom Christians call God. Such seems to be the decided tendency of science and philosophy.

Sacredness of the Individual

The second element is but a corollary of the first—the growing sacredness of the individual. If all life is unified in one supreme life, each individual is enhanced in value because it is a part of the all inclusive and the universal. It partakes of the divine nature, and is to be judged not by what it possesses, but by what it is and by that to which it is related. This thought is as old as the book of Job, for there the writer says: If I have despised the cause of my man-servant or of my maid-servant, when they contended with me; what then shall I do when God riseth up? And when he visiteth, what shall I answer him? Did not he that made me in the womb make him? And did not one fashion us in the womb? Job 31:13-15. This was the supreme teaching of Jesus Christ—out of which grew His universal sympathy—but, strange to say, the Christian Church is just coming to realize the tremendous meaning of this conception.

Social Responsibility

Growing out of these two is the third element of modern social ideals, namely, the sense of responsibility which one man feels for the well-being of all other men. If there is one supreme person—a Father God; if each individual is caught up into that Godhood and so becomes sacred; then, each man is brother to his neighbor, just because they are both alike sons of God —and every true brother must be interested in, and, so far as his power extends, responsible for, the welfare of every other brother in this universal household. Such, it seems to me, is the real meaning of this new social awakening.

Loyalty to Social Ideals

If, then, this is the highest development of human thought—if our philosophy, our science, and our religion have led us to this—that each individual is sacred and we have an obligation to him because of what he is—then, we, who desire to be loyal to the highest, must let this highest find expression in our attitude, in our words, and in our deeds; for, as Dr. Royce has said, "Loyalty, as you see, is essentially an active virtue. It involves manifold sentiments—love good-will, earnestness, delight in the cause, but it is complete only in the motor terms, never in merely sentimental terms. It is useless to call my feelings loyal unless my muscles somehow express my loyalty."[1] The enunciation of a social principle has far-reaching meaning for our present discussion, for if a man is sacred just because he is a human individual, we will need to realize anew that the negro has a claim on our sympathy and help. President King, in his latest volume, has well put it: "We can

[1] "Race Questions and Other American Problems," p. 239.

hardly claim, indeed, to have risen to the level of even the common consciousness of our time, if we are not ready to recognize the ideals of others, though expressed in quite unconventional forms. The willingness to see and to cherish ideals, and the heroism persistently to live or unhesitatingly to die for them, let us be sure, is not confined to our clique or to our race. Have we really open eyes for the hidden ideals in the lives that seem to us unlike our own—laborer, capitalist, negro, white, educated, uneducated, quick or slow? It is not a true interpretation of Christian law of love which insists upon either racial or class barriers to the setting aside of the far more fundamental likeness of men. We owe reverence and faith and love not merely to those whom we call our own, but to all—in the significant words of Jesus, 'despairing of no man' (Luke, 6:35, margin). And we shall have no final peace, either as individuals or as a nation, until we recognize in its entirety this primal law of Jesus."[1]

The Real Question

Now, the real point of the race question is not *shall we have social intermingling—but shall we recognize that the other man has a soul, is a real human personality*—in spite of the fact that he often lives on a back alley, wears poor clothes, uses a broken language, and has a black skin. I have sometimes felt that we really do not believe the negro is possessed of human personality.

---

[1] "Ethics of Jesus," p. 246.

This fact came to me with intensity some years ago as I was riding on a Pullman car through Alabama. We stopped rather long at some small station, and I noted, without asking the cause, that a very large crowd of colored people were gathered on the station platform. After the train had started again, a traveling man, who had gone out to see what was wrong, returned to the car, and was asked by his companion the cause of the delay. "Oh, nothing," replied the drummer, "one 'nigger' shot another, and they were loading the wounded one on to carry him to the nearest town with a hospital." Then and there it dawned upon me that we really did not appreciate the sacredness of humanity, provided that humanity be clothed in a dark skin.

Professor DuBois describes in beautiful and heart-searching English the death of his own baby boy. He tells how dark the day seemed to him as the carriages rolled along through the crowded streets of Atlanta behind the hearse, which carried the lifeless form of the child, as dear to him as life. As the crowd parted for a moment to let the procession pass, some one inquired who it was that had died. Professor DuBois heard the reply as it broke in upon his saddened heart—"Just 'niggers.' " Do you wonder that he is sometimes bitter?

One would be disposed to charge him with over-emphasizing the indifference of white men if we had not lived all our lives in the midst of these conditions and had not heard such expressions hundreds of times. These, of course, are the expressions of the coarser element of white men, and yet they indicate a tendency to forget that a subject race is not a dehumanized race. It should be said also that this attitude toward a weaker race is not seen alone in the South. I have seen things in Northern cities, and heard words to and about foreigners which made my blood boil. When I was making a tour of the Pacific Coast colleges, I saw treatment of Japanese which I could scarcely keep from resenting with physical violence—but I reflected that this was only parallel to the attitude of the coarser element of my own section toward a backward race.

Attitude Toward Dependent Races

Mr. Milligan, in his charming book, "The Jungle Folk of Africa," tells us the story of the treatment of the Kruboys, who load and unload the ships on the West Coast. This work is exceedingly dangerous, on account of poor harbors and heavy surf, and none with less endurance, skill and bravery than these Africans would dare undertake the task.

One day the sea was so very dangerous, "the boys presented themselves in a body before one of the officers and said: 'Mastah, them sea be bad too much. We no be fit for land cargo. S'pose we try, we go loss all cargo, and plenty man's life. So please excuse to-day, Mastah, for we think to-morrow go be fine.'

"The answer they received was a volley of profanity and curses. 'Just because one of them was killed they all turn cowards,' said one. 'Always thinking of themselves,' said another. With many such shrewd observations and sundry moral exhortations to bravery, the boats were lowered and they were ordered into them."

"One day our boys went ashore early in the morning, leaving the ship at half-past five. They were expecting to make the trip before breakfast, as usual, and therefore had nothing to eat before starting. They had landed the cargo safely at the trading-house; but the sea was so bad that they could not get off to the ship all that day. They made several unsuccessful attempts, and it was almost night before they succeeded. Meanwhile, the swell was so heavy that we had steamed far out for safety, and were anchored seven miles from the shore. The boys reached the ship after dark, and we then learned that the white trader ashore had given them nothing to eat, although the ship would have repaid him. Those boys had battled with the sea and with hunger, not having had a taste of food all that day.'

"Only a short time afterwards, one evening at the table, an officer who had been ashore told us a story that was intended to prove the cruelty of the native. A white trader, he said, had caught a young elephant. He went away on a journey to the bush, leaving the care of it to his native workmen. Upon his return, after several months, he found the elephant in very poor health, and a few weeks later it died. There was no doubt that the natives had neglected to feed it in his absence, and this was the cause of its death. Horrible cruelty of the beastly native!

Pungent remarks, appropriate to the occasion, were contributed all around the table. For myself, I was thinking of those starved and tired boys battling with a raging sea. But I said not a word. What would be the use?"

So ever it is that a weak and dependent race is badly used by those that are greedy and unscrupulous. One cannot refrain from calling attention to Christ's parable in Matt. 25:34-46: "Inasmuch as ye did it not unto one of these least, ye did it not unto me." The application of these words to the problem in hand cannot by any possibility be escaped, by the man of open mind.

Test of White Civilization

We have heard much discussion of whether the negro would be able to stand the test of contact with a more advanced civilization. In my opinion this is not at all the real question. The question at issue is, *will the white man, with his superior training, greater advancement, and larger opportunities, be able to stand the test of contact with a less fortunate race?* Every race, as well as every individual, must be finally judged by its attitude toward, and its treatment of, those who are not able to protect themselves. The father that despises one of his children because it is weaker physically or mentally, is branded as a savage. The boy that "picks on" another under his size is promptly denominated a bully and a coward. Not less will the race that deals unfairly with a weaker and more infantile race be judged of God to be unworthy of its heritage. "The responsibility of a privileged people" is the key thought of one of the world's greatest prophetic utterances. "You only have I known of all the families of the earth," said Amos to the highly favored Israelites, "Therefore I will visit upon you all your iniquities."

A National Question

The supreme race questions of this nation are not whether the Chinese and Japanese on the Pacific Coast will be able to meet the demands of a more exacting civilization; not whether the European immigrant of the East is the equal of the native American; not whether the negro of the South can ever measure up to the standard of achievement of his white neighbor — *but whether in all these varying situations we Americans, with our boasted culture, larger wealth, and splendid opportunities, will be able so to deal with these weaker peoples as to prove to God and to the world that we are a race of superior advancement.* Our culture and our civilization are not given us for selfish use. We are simply the custodians of these rich blessings. Just as the new social consciousness demands that a man of accumulated millions shall use it for the good of humanity—so the social sense of the world at large will sooner or later demand that we shall use our culture and our civilization to elevate those less fortunate than ourselves.

Fair Mindedness Toward the Negro

Thus, we have revealed the first great service that we can render to the negro race. We must change public opinion. We must see to it that he is no longer thought of simply as a brute, but as a human being. Here there needs to be discrimination—and the crowd rarely ever discriminates. Because one negro, or a dozen, or two score, or several thousand may be brutish and commit brutal crimes, it is neither fair-minded nor just to accuse the whole race as being without souls. There are many brutal white men. Many of them are as low in sin and shame as human thought can imagine, and yet we assert the essential dignity and sacredness of the individual. If we are to be fair to the negro, we must recognize that there are various stratas within that race, and that many of them are working hard to acquire culture and character. We shall give the race a great impetus when we help the world to recognize that they must have a fair chance—that they must be treated as human personalities.

Obligation to Know the Negro

Another aim we need to set for ourselves is a more thorough knowledge of the negro's condition. Our attention was called, in the first chapter, to the ignorance of our white people concerning negro life. It should be the deliberate purpose of every college man to know more about this problem. This book claims to do nothing but point the way. Each man must investigate for himself. We must go to their homes just to see how they live, we must visit their schools to find how they think, we must visit their churches to know how they worship.

To the man who is in earnest about life there can be no more fascinating study than to find just how this "other half lives." It must always be remembered that this can be done well only in the sympathetic spirit.

Visit Schools and Churches

But we can do much more than investigate conditions. There is the very greatest need for men that have higher ideals to lend their help and encouragement in the matter of education and religion. It would mean much to the negro youth if more white men visited their schools and made addresses that would fire the ambition of these backward children. Character is made by setting ideals—and who can better do this than the educated white men of the South? In like manner, we would do well to speak in their churches, giving them addresses on the practical ethical problems. I cannot imagine a greater service that we could render. In particular, addresses could be given to the men and boys on questions of social purity which might be of very great benefit. I gave such an address recently to a group of negro men, and many of them said afterwards it was the only address of the kind they had ever heard. If we are looking for some practical service, here is the chance.

Negro Sunday Schools

In this connection, one is reminded of the large opportunity for service through the negro Sunday school. There is hardly a negro church

that would not welcome the services of a college man to teach its Bible class for older people,
or to teach a group of younger men, or a class
of boys.   In the city of Nashville, the Methodist
Training School is sending out Bible teachers to
a number of churches.   I have visited some of
these churches, and it was with evident pride and
appreciation that they told me of this help.

In other places there is need for the organization of Sunday schools in those sections of the
city or country where there are no churches.
Hampden-Sidney students have been doing this
for a number of years.   They organize small
schools anywhere within a radius of three or
four miles of the college, and students go out
to teach.

Presbyterian Colored Mission

One of the most notable undertakings of the
kind is that of the Presbyterian Theological Seminary in Louisville, Kentucky.   Rev. John Little,
who was one of the student founders of this
particular Sunday school, and is now in charge
as superintendent, gives the following account
of its inception: "At a business meeting of the
Students' Missionary Society of the Presbyterian
Theological Seminary in Louisville, November,
1897, the needs of the colored people were mentioned, and the suggestion made that a Sunday
school be organized for their instruction.   Six
students volunteered to teach in such a Sunday
school, and plans were formulated to begin the
work.   We thought it would be an easy matter
to secure a house, but we found landlords very

cautious about renting buildings for this purpose. Twenty-five vacant houses were inspected before one could be rented."

"The house was formerly a lottery office, and was well known to the people of the neighborhood. This site was selected because it was in the midst of a densely settled negro district. These negroes were very poor, and day and night were exposed to vice. Saloons were on every corner; gambling places were numerous."

"A definite site on Preston Street—a main thoroughfare—having been selected, the six teachers divided themselves into three groups, going two and two. Each group took a street and visited every house, and in the tenement houses every room. They gave a personal invitation to each member of the family to attend the services and left a printed card giving the name of the mission, the location, and the hours for services. This plan was persistently followed until the building was crowded."

"In the homes we were well received, and invited to come again. In the majority of cases the family promised to attend the next Sunday, 'If I live, and nothing happens.' In nine cases out of ten 'something happened' to the parents, for very few of the older people came to the mission in the early days. In later days they came in larger numbers."

The School Opened

"The doors were opened in February, 1898 and 23 negro pupils were enrolled. Within a month the attendance had grown to 40. Our room was full, and special efforts to secure a larger attendance ceased, and we tried to develop the character of those enrolled."

"The first session of this Sunday school revealed the great need of the people dwelling in this section of the city. Here we found hundreds of children, within the sound of the bells of white and colored churches, who never attended. The pupils were arranged as in an ordinary school. The singing was good, and this natural gift has been developed until the music is excellent. . . ."[1]

This work has grown until, in 1909, there were 450 regular Sunday school students; there were sewing classes for girls, woodwork classes for boys, classes in basketry, cooking, etc. What is fully as important, playgrounds have been arranged where colored boys can go for an afternoon of clean sport. Such a work as this can be reproduced in any city in the South, if only men can be found with large enough faith and sufficient spirit of self-sacrifice.

Famous Examples

For this kind of work we have the very best of precedent in the work of such men as Stonewall Jackson and Robert E. Lee. On one of my visits to Washington and Lee University, I walked out into the country and chanced upon an old man, who had been one of the negro boys in the Sunday school conducted by Jackson before the war, Jackson then being a professor

---

[1] For further facts, address Rev. John Little, 540 Roselane, Louisville, Ky.

at Virginia Military Institute. The old man was very proud of the fact that he sat under the famous General, and quoted a number of Scripture passages to prove that he had profited by such instruction. With such an illustrious example, we can well afford to have our share in such a worthy work.

Helping Colored Young Men's Christian Associations

Again, our colleges located in cities where there are also negro schools, can be of large service by helping to foster the Colored Branch of the Young Men's Christian Association among these colored students. The president of the Young Men's Christian Association in the white college can meet the committees of the colored Association, and give ideas that will be invaluable. This particular suggestion comes to me from a negro, the president of a negro college, and from a Christian worker among his students. In like manner, men can help in carrying on the Bible study work of the Young Men's Christian Association. I made a visit a year or two ago to Carlisle Indian School, Carlisle, Pa., and while there, we enrolled four hundred Indian students in Bible study. There were no students in the school sufficiently prepared to lead these classes. We, therefore, secured leaders from Dickinson College and Dickinson Seminary to go over once each week and do this work. Why should not the students of the South, who believe that the negro student should know the Bible, go out to these schools to conduct Association classes?

Athletic Help, etc.

Another place where the white students may serve the colored is in athletics. As a rule, the negro school is not able to employ coaches or to secure desirable officials for games. And there is no greater need in the negro school than a genuine athletic life. Those of us that have defended athletics in our own schools on the basis of their moral influence, and of their physical uplift, must readily understand that the colored student needs this even more. At Vanderbilt University, athletic men have gone out to Fisk, Roger Williams, and Meharry for years to act as officials in such games, and wherever I have chanced upon one of the students of these institutions, they have always had a most kindly feeling toward all Vanderbilt men. There is no surer way to settle the race question than in these small matters to indicate our interest in these men, and our willingness to help them.

Boy's Clubs

In like manner, university students can be of the greatest service to the boys of the negro race if they will organize them into clubs and give them a chance to have some clean and wholesome fun. One of the most serious difficulties in connection with the negro problem is the fact that there are no playgrounds, no places of amusement for these boys. A colored boy cannot play ball, he cannot play tennis, he cannot go to a gymnasium, he cannot go swimming in the city —because there is no place open to him. A few years ago some colored men rented a small park in Atlanta for the sake of having ball games for colored boys. But some white man in the vicinity complained, and the park was closed by the city officials. A colored man in Atlanta told me that there was not a single decent place of amusement, so far as he knew, where negroes could go. No wonder we are turning out crops of criminals. A negro boy is just like a white boy—he has the play instinct. If this instinct is not legitimately gratified, he is either stunted by too constant work and no play, or else he is demoralized by no work, no play, and all loafing. I believe some of these conditions can be righted by our college men and our churches. If we will organize negro boys' clubs, where these boys can be brought together for military training, or for simple games, or for any type of amusement that is wholesome, together with such other more serious and helpful activities as may seem wise, we may bring great blessing to the whole race.

Reform Schools Needed

In this connection, it should be said that reform schools have been established for delinquent white boys in most States; but the colored boy who commits a petty crime is thrust right in with the most hardened criminals, and is soon turned out with criminal instincts. From the standpoint of economy alone, this is poor policy, for the boy that becomes a criminal is a constant burden on the State, when he might have been saved to the State for a real factor in production.

Racial Integrity

One cannot refrain from saying a word here about that other crying evil which is the plague of white and black alike. Much has been said about the horrors of an unnamable crime perpetrated by negro men. The negro race, as a whole, condemns this, and all the better classes are helping in the detection and prosecution of the criminals. But I have had more than one honest and worthy negro man tell me that we would never put a stop to this crime until white men ceased their ravages of colored girls. Of course, it cannot be denied that many colored girls court the favor of white men, but the white man is the stronger, and should be held most responsible. But this is only one side of the question. There is another and a blacker side. A college president recently told me of a case which was enough to make one's blood boil. A negro drayman, after giving his daughter all the training possible at home, sent her away to the Prairie View Normal, in Texas, where she graduated, having in mind teaching as a life work. Meanwhile, an unscrupulous, but wealthy, white man became attracted by her looks and followed her back to her small Mississippi town in the attempt to persuade her to return with him as his personal slave. The father of this girl went to my friend, the white college president, and asked him what to do. Said he: "This white man is hanging about trying to rob my daughter of her purity. If I kill him, I will be mobbed in an hour, and if I let him alone, I may lose the hope and pride of a lifetime." No wonder the colored man rebels at such an unjust situation.

Negro Testimony

At a meeting held in Atlanta, to which I have referred in the introduction of this book, the hardest charge brought against the white man by the negro delegates present was the fact that many negro girls who would withstand the appeals of negro men were helpless, and lost their virtue to white men who employed them or who might have enough money to turn their simple heads.

The Blackest Crime

There has been no small talk about social equality. I do not believe in social intermingling, nor do the best class of negroes. But where a white man uses his larger power and influence to force a negro girl to give up her purity, there is no question of social equality involved; the man is so infinitely below the level of the girl that he does not deserve to be mentioned in the same breath. It is a crime as black as night when a man robs a white girl of her purity, even though she consents—but she is his equal in moral strength and has powers of self-protection. The negro girl, however, has no such equal chance in the struggle; so, when a white man takes advantage of one who is socially down, who cannot protect herself, he is a fiend of the blackest die. There is need that college men should create a sentiment of condemnation against such diabolical sin. If we expect the black man to respect our women—and he must—then we must force our white men to keep hands off the negro girl—whether she be pure or impure. There must not be any mingling of the races.

Lynching

Just here one must say a word about the question of lynching. It is a fact that it grows more prevalent in both North and South. The question is, can it be defended? and if not, can it be stopped? In the first place, what is the effect on the colored community of lynching? Does it act as a deterrent of further crime? Not at all. I have talked with a great many negro men, and, so far as a white man can, have got into the spirit and mode of their thought on this subject. Lynching only maddens and enrages the lower class. They look upon the lynched negro as a martyr, who has laid down his life on the altar of a just hatred of his oppressor. I am absolutely convinced that lynching does not frighten the criminal class, and hence does not prevent the awful crime against our women. On the other hand, it has increased this crime, and has put the criminal in the class of martyrs. If we love our women and want to protect them, some less spectacular method of punishment must be devised.

It Degrades the White Man

What effect does lynching have on the whole community? Bad, and only bad. There is no light to relieve the shadow here. Whenever men, in the name of law and justice, so far forget themselves as to trample every law under their feet, and, in their mad frenzy, even take the lives of honest officials who heroically stand out for their duty and for the law; when, in their mad brutality, they burn or hang or riddle with bullets a wretched criminal supposed to be guilty of this crime — though it occasionally happens that he is not—just so often is the self-respect of the community lowered, and the sacredness of law is broken down. The effect is brutalizing and demoralizing. The result of this disregard for law is seen on every hand. It comes out in the night riding in Kentucky, in the Reel Foot Lake tragedies in Tennessee, and in numerous other ways. As we sow, so shall we reap. If we sow mobs, and violence, and disrespect for courts of justice, we shall surely reap murders, lawlessness and debased public opinion. This is a very high price to pay for the luxury of a little bloodthirsty revenge.

Does not Prevent Publicity

But some one says that we cannot afford to humiliate our women by bringing them into public for the trial of the criminal. No, surely not, but the trial can be conducted with closed doors. Would this be more humiliating than what now takes place? Does not the infuriated mob take the criminal before the victim if she is alive and ask her to identify him? There is no privacy, no decorum, not even lack of publicity. Nothing could be more public, nothing could be

more revolting to real womanhood than our
present methods.

Defeats Justice

And, last of all, justice cannot be done by a
frenzied mob. In a Republic such as ours, every
man is supposed to have the right of a trial, the
right to defend himself against false accusations.
A mob never reasons, it does not weigh evidence,
it simply acts in the madness of its fury. I quote
a case in point: "William McArthur has been
for many years the janitor of a white church in
a former slave State. He owns a farm and city
house; has a bank account, and could loan
money more easily than most of the church members he serves. His reputation for character is
as good as theirs. When, therefore, a disrep-
utable white woman attempted to blackmail him
by threatening to charge him with assault on a
child, he naturally went to the church officers for
advice. They believed in him as they did in
each other, but put him on a midnight train for
California. To his Northern pastor it was in-
credible that a man of his reputation should have
to flee like a thief. The answer was: 'This
community is likely to lynch first and investigate
afterwards.' So McArthur went—he could
afford to—saying, with pathetic humor, 'I always wanted to travel West, anyhow.' After six
months he felt safe to come back and take up
his work. Not long after the community did
lynch three negroes on an Easter morning. The
grand jury, investigating afterward, found that
two of them were certainly innocent. Only bay-

onets saved the negro quarter from burning.
Then McArthur came to his pastor to know
where, under the stars and stripes, a self-respecting and respected black man could buy his own
vine and fig tree, and go and sit down under
them in the ordinary security of Christian civilization."

"Now McArthur's character is fixed so that
adversity, while it seams his brow and weights
his steps, does not make a social rebel of him;
but his boy, when I last saw him, was behind
the bars."

"Now, I charge that America did not give
McArthur's boy a square deal. Of course, he
is a responsible soul, with heart, will and conscience enough to make some impression on his
own moral destiny. Let him bear his full share
of the blame; but let us weigh this: he had felt
the helplessness of the property-owning negro
before the blackmailer; had seen his father a
fugitive at midnight, his life hanging upon an
idle word; *had heard just men confess their in-
ability to protect one in whom they had all confidence;* had vainly longed for a fatherland which
could guarantee somewhere a peaceful death to
one who had lived in honor; had smelled the
burning flesh of innocent men of his own race.
Besides all this, his own weakness had been
trafficked in by a venal police power. Such
things are not calculated to make a young negro
into a model citizen. You tell me that after all
the cord and the torch are rare, that statistically
one is more likely to die from falling off a step-
ladder at home than a negro is to be lynched. I

reply that when one has once come under the shadow of such a tragedy he can never forget it. It stamps his imagination for all time and sears his soul against the social order in which it is tolerated." [1]

Sentiment Against Lynching Needed

It is ours to create a sentiment of justice, of respect for law, of reverence for the authority of the courts. No nation can stand where its law is not respected and where any chance mob rises up and in the name of justice breaks every law of the land, and tramples justice under its feet.

Justice in Petty Crimes

The negro should get justice, not only in this respect, but also in petty crimes. We need to use our influence here to see that he does get justice. He needs justice in the courts, but he does not get it; far too infrequently he is treated leniently because his white friend pleads his cause, and again, too frequently, he has no chance because there is no friend at court. Whatever may be said to the contrary, the negro does not get full justice at the bar of the law.

Justice in Public Conveyances

Neither does he get fair treatment in many public conveyances. I once asked Prof. John Wesley Gilbert, one of the best educated and most thoroughly Christian negroes in the South, what he thought of the "Jim Crow" laws. His

---

[1] "Christian Reconstruction in the South," pp. 204-5.

reply was that he had no objection to them if they were fairly administered. But, of course, they are not. We all know that. Some cheap, white man who happens to be in authority treats the negro with disrespect and abuses him, lest some one may think that he, the conductor, is not better than they. Professor Gilbert told me he never rode on the car with his wife, lest some cheap conductor might insult her, and he would do as any other man, defend her, and a mob would be the result. This is not justice, it is not humanity, it is not Christianity. We must change it.

Negro Self-Sufficiency

Lastly, if we are to have perfect distinctness of life in this section, we must make the negro sufficient unto himself. So long as all honor lies in being associated with the white man, the negro will want social intermingling. So long as there are none of his own race that can meet him on a high plane and can satisfy the longings of his soul, just so long will he be driven to seek fellowship with white men. But build him up, make him sufficient in himself, give him within his own race life that which will satisfy, and the social question will be solved. The cultivated negro is less and less inclined to lose himself and his race in the sea of another race. As he develops, he is finding a new race consciousness, he is building a new race pride. He no longer objects to being called a negro—it is becoming the badge of his race and the mark of his self-sufficiency. We have nothing, therefore, to fear from giving him a chance. With every new chance he becomes more satisfied to live his life within the pale of his own race. If ever the negro is to become an efficient workman and a real economic factor, it will be because he has so far been elevated in his desires and needs that only constant labor can satisfy his wants. We shall increase his efficiency by increasing his wants. If ever he is to become a good citizen, it will be because he has been so elevated as to desire decency and honor, and not because he fears the law if he lives otherwise. If he is to be kept as a separate and distinct race, without any desire to mingle in social life with the white race, it will be by making his race so self-sufficient that he can find his desires, his ambitions, his social longings satisfied within his own ranks. This must come through the elevation of the whole race.

We Need not Fear Advancement

We have nothing to fear from the advancement of the negroes. It is a poor race which can sustain the position it has won only by forever crowding down other races that come into competition with itself. For my part, I do not believe the white race need take any such position. We shall be able to hold our own and care for our own, however great the advancement of the negro race may be. Rather, my fear is that the negro race in the South will remain so backward, that it will remain so ignorant, that it will remain so far in the rear of civilization, that we of the South will forever be held down by the weight of our helpless neighbors, and allow the people of other sections of our country to march on and leave us hopelessly behind in our wealth, in our civilization, and in our culture.

Negro Needs Encouragement

Let us encourage the negro race to advance as rapidly as possible; let us give him all the chance we can. He does not need to be held back or discouraged; he needs to be cheered on. He needs to have held before him the records of high endeavor. No boy has ever grown great by believing that his life was worthless and his ability below the average. No race will ever become useful and industrious by being browbeaten and discouraged. However difficult the task, we must bring the negro to believe in himself. We must make him feel that he is capable of being a true man. We must help him to become sufficient unto himself. Any other course on our part is the madness of a slow suicide, for we rise or fall with the moral power of our section.

Will We Stand the Test

Ours is, perhaps, the most difficult task that has been set before the people of any section of America. It will require more patience, it will cost more faith, it will need more persistence, it will demand a truer sympathy, and it will require more Christian courage to solve this great question than any other question that faces the American people. If we are faithless in this trust, woe be to ourselves and our successors!

But if we are faithful, the very difficulty of our task will mean a greater manhood and a brighter glory than a lesser task could give. I have faith that the educated men of the South will not bewail their fate, but that they will, with the strength of men, meet and master these stupendous difficulties. *It is not the negro that is on trial before the world, but it is we, the white men of the South.* The world is looking on to see whether we shall have sufficient wisdom, sufficient courage, sufficient Christian spirit to lend a helping hand to the race that is down. May the spirit of the Christ, the Friend of Men, give us strength to stand the test.

BIBLIOGRAPHY

The volumes listed in this bibliography are some of the best in print. The word of explanation after each title has not been intended in a critical spirit, but to help those who only care to purchase one or two volumes to secure the ones which will best meet their needs. Each volume here listed has been carefully read for this purpose.—W. D. W.

Atlanta University Publications (Atlanta University Press, 1896-1906) :

No. 1, Mortality among Negroes in Cities, 1896.
Mortality among Negroes in Cities, 1903.
2, Social and Physical Condition of Negroes in Cities, 1897.
3, Some Efforts of Negroes for Social Betterment, 1898.
4, The Negro in Business, 1899.
5, The College Bred Negro, 1900 (two editions).
6, The Negro Common School, 1901.
7, The Negro Artisan, 1902.
8, The Negro Church, 1903.
9, Notes on Negro Crime, 1904.
10, A Select Bibliography of the Negro American, 1905.
11, Health and Physique of the Negro American, 1906.

These are the most thorough and original investigations of the negro problem that have been made.

BRYCE, JAMES. "The Relation of the Advanced and the Backward Races of Mankind." Clarendon Press, 1903. A clear statement of the conditions under which races amalgamate and those under which racial integrity prevails.

* BAKER, RAY STANNARD. "Following the Color Line." Doubleday, Page & Co., 1908. A clear, fair statement of race conditions, as seen by a Northern man on an extended tour through the South; perhaps the sanest book on the topic by a Northern man.

COMMONS, JOHN R. "Races and Immigrants in America." The Macmillan Company, 1908.

DUBOIS, W. E. B. "The Souls of Black Folk." A. C. McClurg & Co., 1907. From the standpoint of one of the most cultured and literary colored men in America. It bears the marks of keen insight into the thought of the race—at times bitterly pessimistic.

DOUGLASS, H. PAUL. "Christian Reconstruction in the South." The Pilgrim Press, 1909. A study of the work of the American Missionary Association in the South.

DOWD, JEROME. "The Negro Races." The Macmillan Company, 1907. A scholarly study of three of the five great divisions of the negro race in Africa.

*DUNBAR, PAUL LAURENCE. "Lyrics of Lowly Life." Dodd, Mead & Co., 1896. Poems that catch the spirit of the old-time "darkey" to a remarkable degree. Likewise his poems of Cabin and Field, etc.

GROGMAN. "Progress of a Race." J. L. Nichols & Co., 1907. A running account of the life of the American Negro—not all too accurate.

HART, ALBERT BUSHNELL. "The Southern South." Appleton, 1910.

HELM, MARY. "The Upward Path." Young People's Missionary Movement, 1909. A very sane statement by a Southern woman who writes with clear insight and with deep sympathy for the negro's struggle.

HOFFMAN, FREDERICK L. "Race Traits and Tendencies of the American Negro." American Economic Association. Published by Macmillan & Co., 1896. The most scholarly and exhaustive study yet made of population, vital statistics, anthropometry, and race amalgamation.

HARRISON & BARNES. "The Gospel among the Slaves." Smith & Lamar, Nashville, Tenn., 1893. A careful compilation of facts concerning the evangelization of the negro during days of slavery.

MILLER, KELLY. "Race Adjustment." The Neale Publishing Company, 1908. Strictly reliable as to facts, showing deep insight into the life of the race; a little critical of the white man.

*MIRRIAM, GEORGE S. "The Negro and the Nation." Young People's Missionary Movement, 1906. A historical statement of the political questions arising out of slavery.

*MURPHY, EDGAR GARDINER. "The Present South." Longmans, Green & Co., 1904. The best expression of the spirit of the New South, dealing with many phases of the Negro question.

"The Basis of Ascendency." Longmans, Green & Co., 1909. An "explicit statement of those fundamental principles of policy" which underlie the solution of the race question. Absolutely fair and Christian in spirit.

NASSAU, ROBERT HAMILL. "Fetichism in West Africa." Charles Scribner's Sons, 1904. A most entertaining and thorough statement of the religious life and practices of the West African negro.

*PAGE, THOMAS NELSON. "The Negro, the Southerner's Problem." Charles Scribner's Sons, 1904. Characterized by thorough familiarity with the "old-time" negro, with less accurate knowledge of present conditions. Prone to magnify all the virtues of the slave, and all the vices of the present negro.

ROYCE, JOSIAH. "Race Questions, Provincialism, and Other American Problems." The Macmillan Company, 1908. It is tolerably certain that few Southern men will accept Professor Royce's statement that race antipathies are on a "level with a dread of snakes and of mice." The volume can hardly be called unbiased or scholarly.

SHANNON, A. H. "Racial Integrity." Smith & Lamar, Nashville, Tenn., and Dallas, Texas, 1907. A study of race amalgamation and other topics.

SINCLAIR, WILLIAM A. "The Aftermath of Slavery." Small, Maynard & Co., 1905. Somewhat unfair in its treatment of the question. The author is a colored man who chafes under present conditions.

SMITH, WILLIAM BENJAMIN. "The Color Line." McClure, Phillips & Co., 1904. Brilliant in its statements, but bitter in its sarcasm. It is doubtful if the conclusions reached as to the future decay of the negro will prove true.

THOMAS, WILLIAM HANNIBAL. "The American Negro." The Macmillan Company, 1901. The harshest arraignment of the race by one of its own members. While showing clear insight into negro character, it is certainly unfair.

WASHINGTON & DuBois. "The Negro in the South." George W. Jacobs & Co., 1907. Dealing with the economic and religious life of the negro.

*WASHINGTON, BOOKER T. "Up from Slavery." Doubleday, Page & Co., 1907. An autobiography of the writer, full of interest, and written in the finest spirit.

    "Working with Hands." Doubleday, Page & Co., 1904. A splendid story of the Tuskegee Institute and a powerful argument for industrial education.

    "Character Building." Doubleday, Page & Co., 1903.

    Chapel Talks by B. T. Washington at Tuskegee Institute.

*The Y. P. M. M., New York, has published a set of seven volumes on the Negro question, price $5. This set includes the volumes marked with a star, and "Daybreak in the Dark Continent," by Naylor.

Race Relationships in the South

Vol. 1. Negro Life in the South,
W. D. Weatherford.
Vol. 2. Up from Slavery, Booker T. Washington.
Vol. 3. ⎰ The Story of the Negro,
Vol. 4. ⎱ Booker T. Washington.
Vol. 5. The Basis of Ascendency,
Edgar Gardner Murphy.
Vol. 6. Race Distinctions in American Law,
Gilbert Thomas Stephenson.
Vol. 7. The Southern South, Albert Bushnell Hart.

This Library of seven volumes deals with the political, economic, social, educational, moral and religious aspects of the race problems.

It brings together the work of some of the greatest leaders in this realm of thought, chosen out of the scores of volumes printed in the last ten years. In scholarly accuracy, statesmanlike outlook, and fairmindedness toward all concerned, this library constitutes the ripest, sanest and most sympathetic statement of these problems. Price in original bindings, $9.75; in this special set, $5.00, carriage collect.

Introducing Men to Christ

W. D. Weatherford.   Cloth, .50

This volume attempts to make clear to men the steps which one takes in entering the Christian life, the results in one's life of becoming a Christian, the fundamental message of Christianity as compared with other religions, and the foundation stones upon which the Christian faith rests. Two chapters study how this message of the Christian life may be passed on to one's friends. Ten studies of seven sections each for daily study in the fundamental question of Christian life.

ASSOCIATION PRESS - - - NEW YORK

Helpful for Life and Service

MANHOOD OF THE MASTER
Harry Emerson Fosdick   Art leather, 50 cents

This little volume will lead to a better understanding and deeper appreciation of the Master's character as an individual. The significant events of His life are considered, but only as they illuminate His personality. Arranged for individual use and for Bible study groups.

PAUL IN EVERYDAY LIFE
John Douglas Adam   Art leather, 50 cents

A companion volume to the widely used "Christ in Everyday Life." Daily readings from the epistles with personal applications.

CHRIST IN EVERYDAY LIFE
E. I. Bosworth   Art leather, 50 cents

Daily Bible readings with comment. "The aim is to help the reader in his daily devotions, and in this the work is entirely successful, more so than any other we have seen."   —*Student World*.

PRESENT FORCES IN NEGRO PROGRESS
W. D. Weatherford   Cloth, 50 cents

A fair-minded statement of conditions as they are. Intended to meet the supreme need of the hour for facts rather than theories. Supplemented by an excellent bibliography and index.

IMMIGRANT RACES IN NORTH AMERICA
Peter Roberts   Cloth, 50 cents

An illustrated study of the home environment and historic background of the twelve chief nationalities from which immigration is drawn. A necessary handbook for industrial workers and equally valuable for the general reader. An encyclopedia of the history—religious, political and social—that explains present conditions.

SOCIAL ACTIVITIES FOR MEN AND BOYS
A. M. Chesley   Cloth, Illustrated, $1.00

Plain directions for catching cheerfulness. A manual of games, amateur shows, outings, innings, and other things that will raise a wholesome breeze in any social circle. The material came from all good sources available and has all been successfully tested.

ASSOCIATION PRESS - NEW YORK